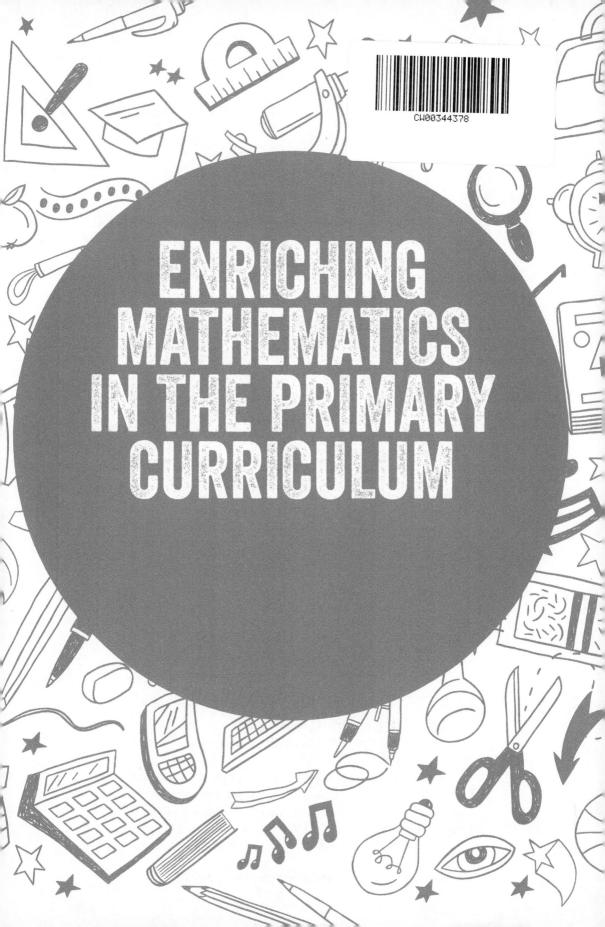

ENRICHING MATHEMATICS IN THE PRIMARY CURRICULUM

Sara Miller McCune founded SAGE Publishing in 1965 to support the dissemination of usable knowledge and educate a global community. SAGE publishes more than 1000 journals and over 800 new books each year, spanning a wide range of subject areas. Our growing selection of library products includes archives, data, case studies and video. SAGE remains majority owned by our founder and after her lifetime will become owned by a charitable trust that secures the company's continued independence.

Los Angeles | London | New Delhi | Singapore | Washington DC | Melbourne

ENRICHING MATHEMATICS IN THE PRIMARY CURRICULUM

SUE POPE
PABLO MAYORGA

SAGE | LearningMatters

Learning Matters
An imprint of SAGE Publications Ltd
1 Oliver's Yard
55 City Road
London EC1Y 1SP

SAGE Publications Inc.
2455 Teller Road
Thousand Oaks, California 91320

SAGE Publications India Pvt Ltd
B 1/I 1 Mohan Cooperative Industrial Area
Mathura Road
New Delhi 110 044

SAGE Publications Asia-Pacific Pte Ltd
3 Church Street
#10-04 Samsung Hub
Singapore 049483

© 2019 Sue Pope and Pablo Mayorga

First published in 2019

Apart from any fair dealing for the purposes of research or private study, or criticism or review, as permitted under the Copyright, Designs and Patents Act 1988, this publication may be reproduced, stored or transmitted in any form, or by any means, only with the prior permission in writing of the publishers, or in the case of reprographic reproduction, in accordance with the terms of licences issued by the Copyright Licensing Agency. Enquiries concerning reproduction outside those terms should be sent to the publishers.

Editor: Amy Thornton
Senior project editor: Chris Marke
Project management: Deer Park Productions
Marketing manager: Lorna Patkai
Cover design: Wendy Scott
Typeset by: C&M Digitals (P) Ltd, Chennai, India
Printed in the UK

Library of Congress Control Number: 2018965496

British Library Cataloguing in Publication Data

A catalogue record for this book is available from the British Library.

ISBN 978-1-5264-8827-5
ISBN 978-1-5264-8826-8 (pbk)

At SAGE we take sustainability seriously. Most of our products are printed in the UK using responsibly sourced papers and boards. When we print overseas we ensure sustainable papers are used as measured by the PREPS grading system. We undertake an annual audit to monitor our sustainability.

CONTENTS

Contents

ABOUT THE EDITORS AND CONTRIBUTORS

THE EDITORS

Sue Pope was Associate Head of School for Teacher Education and Professional Development at Manchester Metropolitan University until 2018. For five years she was the national lead for Mathematics 5-19 at the Qualifications and Curriculum Authority (QCA) where she managed and quality assured substantial research, development and evaluation projects.

She moved to QCA after ten years in higher education working with beginning primary and secondary teachers on undergraduate and postgraduate courses, and supporting experienced teachers working towards higher degrees through researching their own practice. She worked as a local authority advisor after teaching for ten years in a number of schools, including five years as head of mathematics in an 11-18 mixed comprehensive school where she worked closely with feeder primary schools initiating strategies for enabling primary-secondary transition and cross-phase approaches to assessment.

Sue is a long-standing active member of the Association of Teachers of Mathematics and was treasurer until 2018.

Pablo Mayorga is Senior Lecturer in Mathematics Education and Assistant Programme Convener PGCE School Direct at University of Roehampton, London. After completing a PGCE, he worked as a primary school teacher for eight years in schools in south London. During this time he completed a Master's in Mathematics Education at King's College London.

Prior to taking up his current post, he worked in a Teaching School as Research Lead and Specialist Leader of Education (SLE). In this role, he worked with partner schools to establish Lesson Study in mathematics to support teachers' professional development. He also led his school's participation in the Higher Order Mathematics New Curriculum Lesson Study Program funded by the London Schools Excellence Fund.

His research interests are children's development of rational numbers and proportional reasoning.

THE CONTRIBUTORS

Alison Borthwick is a mathematics advisor, lecturer, researcher, qualified teacher, author and learner. Her career has spanned primary, secondary, HEI and advisory roles. She is the current chair of the primary Association of Teachers of Mathematics and Mathematical Association group, a member of the primary contact group for the Advisory Committee on Mathematics Education, and a member of the Early Childhood Mathematics Group. She is also a STEM ambassador and a governor.

Alison is co-author of *Reasons to Reason in Primary Maths and Science* (2018), *Connecting Primary Maths and Science* (2016) and *Curious Learners in Primary Maths, Science, Computing and DT* (2016). In addition she has written numerous articles for UK and international journals, and has presented papers around the world.

Diana Cobden worked as a primary mathematics coordinator for 15 years before becoming a Mathematics Advisor in Dorset. During her four-year teacher training she was very much influenced by publications such as the *Plowden Report, Primary Children and their Education*, because this highlighted a move towards thinking about how children learn as well as what they learn, particularly in mathematics, and this made her determined to make mathematics more accessible and interesting to children. During this time she was involved with the problem-solving element of the national Primary Mathematics Project.

Diana's time as a Mathematics Advisor coincided with the introduction of the National Curriculum and when working with teachers she encouraged them to develop a more open-ended approach in the classroom and to move away from the more formal textbook work they had done previously.

Since retirement Diana has written a number of books including: *Maths from Maps and Plans*; *ICT Numeracy Links*; *Including Low Achievers in the Maths Lesson*; *Thinking by Numbers*; *Measures at Key Stage 2*; *Mad Maths*.

Tony Cotton started his career teaching mathematics in secondary schools in Sheffield. He then worked as an advisory teacher for anti-racist and multicultural education in Leicester before spending time with three commercial publishers. He has taught on secondary and primary teacher education courses in Nottingham and Leeds, becoming Head of the School of Education and Childhood at Leeds Metropolitan University (now Leeds Beckett). In 2012 he left the university sector to work full time as a writer and freelance educational consultant. His publications include *Understanding and Teaching Primary Mathematics* and *Oxford International Primary Mathematics*, a primary mathematics programme for international schools. Tony is the editor of *Mathematics Teaching* and a lifelong member of the Association of Teachers of Mathematics. Tony and Helen Toft regularly work together running workshops on teaching mathematics through drama. They have taught together for nearly 30 years and have been married for 27 years.

Abigail Gosling is senior lecturer and course coordinator for the Early Childhood Education degree at the University of Bedfordshire. She has taught on the Early Years Initial Teacher Education course and across a number of degree programmes in the School of Education and English Language.

Abigail worked as a local authority advisor for seven years, supporting teaching and learning across Early Years provision in maintained, private and voluntary settings. She led the team of teachers in children's centres, supporting pedagogy and professional development. She was the moderation manager for the Early Years Foundation Stage Profile (EYFSP), and worked on the EYFSP Registered Moderator Assessment programme for the Qualifications and Curriculum Development Agency.

Abigail has worked as a teacher for many years in a range of schools and settings, and has learnt so much from the children she taught. Abigail is a member of the Association for Professional Development in Early Years (TACTYC).

Ray Huntley is a mathematics educator with 18 years' experience in teaching and school leadership in the UK and Australia. He has been a mathematics lecturer in Initial Teacher Education since 2002. He is an active member of the Association for Teachers of Mathematics (ATM), the Mathematical Association (MA) and the British Society for Research into Learning Mathematics. He has served as a trustee of ATM and the MA.

Ray is the author of various academic journal and teachers' periodical articles, and he has reviewed many teacher education titles. He completed his doctorate in primary mathematics education studying teachers' subject knowledge and choice of examples. He has worked with many primary schools in different areas of the UK, leading day courses and twilight sessions in mathematics, thinking skills and problem solving. He likes to combine his love of mathematics with his hobbies of games, football, drumming and travel.

Ruth James is Deputy Headteacher at a large primary school in Kingston upon Thames. Her teaching career in primary education has included a local authority mathematics advisory role as well as being a mathematics specialist teacher. She has written articles for *Mathematics Teaching* (ATM's journal) and very much enjoys the role of teacher-researcher. Ruth is passionate about children enjoying their mathematics learning and enabling all children to apply their mathematical skills and knowledge to real-life problem solving.

Sarah Lister is a senior lecturer at Manchester Metropolitan University, co-ordinating the modern foreign languages provision within the primary initial teacher education programmes. She also teaches on the MA in Language Education, exploring some of the key issues associated with language learning, including: motivation; early language learning; effective assessment strategies; and transition between primary and secondary.

Sarah's research and academic enterprise include motivation, early language learning, using technology in the language classroom and Content and Language Integrated Learning (CLIL). She first became interested and involved in CLIL in 2008 after attending her first CLIL conference in Tallinn, Estonia. In June 2010, she successfully secured external funding from Linked Up, a branch of the Association for Language Learning, to lead a European CLIL project. The focus of the research project was to examine the impact of CLIL on pupils' attitudes and motivation. The final project report published in 2012 along with resources and planning documentation are accessible on the Linked Up website at: http://www.links intolanguages.ac.uk/resources/2564.

Josh Lury has taught for 15 years and is passionate about lessons that inspire deep thinking, creativity and reasoning. He studied mathematics and philosophy at the University of Edinburgh, specializing in philosophy for the final two years of his study.

He now works as a writer and consultant, including a role with the Maths Hub in Cornwall, where he lives with his partner and their two boys, both of whom peek over his shoulder while he writes.

Josh is a Mathematics Specialist Teacher and has worked in special schools and secondary schools but has spent most of his time teaching in primary. He is the author of numerous mathematics and English books and resources, including *A Creative Approach to Teaching Calculation* (Bloomsbury) and *Understanding and Teaching Grammar in the Primary Classroom* (Routledge).

Maria McArdle is a Senior Lecturer at the School of Teacher Education, University of Bedfordshire, where she lectures in primary mathematics education on the undergraduate and post-graduate course and also leads the primary PGCE course. She is an active committee member of the Primary Mathematical Association/Association for Teachers of Mathematics group and presents Royal Institute masterclasses in Cambridge.

Beginning her career in computing, Maria moved into education and her previous experience includes playgroup leader, primary teacher, head teacher, local authority mathematics advisor and working with adults with complex needs. Maria is passionate about learning through 'doing' – play and outdoor learning – and enjoys incorporating this into her work.

Cherri Moseley taught for over 15 years in infant and primary schools before moving into consultancy and advisory work. She is an active member of the Mathematical Association and is one of the editors of its popular journal *Primary Mathematics*. Cherri is particularly interested in the use of story and other cross-curricular approaches to inspire learners of mathematics and their teachers. She has written a variety of mathematics resources for teachers, working with and advising a range of publishers. Cherri is also a Mathematics Specialist Teacher and an NCETM (National Centre for Excellence in the Teaching of Mathematics) Professional Development Lead (Primary).

Mike Ollerton taught in primary and secondary schools for 24 years, in ITE for ten years and has been an independent consultant since 2006. As Head of Mathematics in an 11-16 comprehensive school from 1986-95, he led a department that taught in all-attainment classes from Year 7 to Year 11 using problem solving, and enquiry-based approaches without textbooks.

Mike is passionate about making mathematics accessible, stimulating and enjoyable for all; using a wide range of active, practical, enquiry-based approaches based upon simple starting points with many extensions. Mike is a long-standing member of the Association for Teachers of Mathematics, having served for ten years on its General Council, and is a strong advocate for institutional membership.

Mike has written many books including: *Learning and Teaching Mathematics without a Textbook, Everyone is Special, Functioning Mathematically, Creating Positive Classrooms, The Mathematics Teacher's Handbook* and *Getting the Buggers to Add Up.*

Pauline Palmer was the Primary Mathematics Subject Leader at Manchester Metropolitan University (MMU) until 2018. She taught on the undergraduate and post graduate teaching training programmes and was the award co-ordinator for the STEM Master's programme. Her research interests include change management and mathematics pedagogy. Always interested in the use of talk in the mathematics classroom, she became interested in Content and Language Integrated Learning (CLIL) pedagogy from working with a visiting academic from Cordoba in 2013, which led to collaboration with Sarah Lister.

They have since run a series of CLIL-based workshops for local teachers to begin to explore how mathematics can be used as the content focus and context for a CLIL-based approach. Since 2014, they have also been engaged in planning and delivering CLIL training and support for a number of European teachers.

Sarah and Pauline are keen to explore the synergies between mathematics and MFL (Modern Foreign Languages) and how CLIL can be used as an effective pedagogical tool to enhance linguistic and cognitive development in both mathematics and MFL.

Jennie Pennant is an independent mathematics leadership coach and consultant. She was the Professional Development Primary lead at NRICH for four years, following a number of years as the Professional Development Manager at Be a Mathematician (BEAM). Hence Jennie is passionate about empowering school professional learning communities to support children to develop as confident, competent and enthusiastic young mathematicians who are flexible problem solvers with skills appropriate for the challenges of the twenty-first century.

From 2012 to 2015, Jennie was a member of the national Advisory Committee for Mathematics Education (ACME), leading its pro-active work on teachers' professional development. Jennie's research focus is on what constitutes effective CPD for teachers and she has a particular interest in the impact of specialist coaching. She has wide experience in writing, teaching and advising on mathematics both in the UK and abroad. Jennie has taught in both primary and secondary schools.

Suja Sivadasan is a Senior Lecturer at the University of Roehampton, where she teaches primary mathematics on the SCITT (School Centred Initial Teacher Training), PGCE and BA primary education courses and carries out research that supports children's learning of mathematics. Suja is committed to promoting the reasoning process in making mathematical connections and believes that this starts simply by talking about the mathematics. Suja has Key Stage 1 and Key Stage 2 teaching experience in primary schools across Kent and Wiltshire, including as a Numbers Count Teacher. Suja came into primary education after a career in public policy research. She has a doctorate in engineering from the University of Oxford and her undergraduate degree is in engineering from the University of Cambridge. Suja is a member of the Association for Teachers of Mathematics General Council, where she aims to promote the teaching and learning of primary mathematics to enthuse and support primary teachers as mathematicians.

Karen Wilding is an independent primary mathematics consultant supporting schools across the UK and internationally. Having taught for over twenty years in the primary sector and led school improvement as an Early Years advisor and local authority mathematics consultant, she brings a wealth of understanding and first-hand experience to her role.

Karen is an active member of the ATM, MA and NAMA (National Association of Mathematics Advisers) mathematics' associations while also working in a wider capacity with educators and organizations wishing to improve the quality of learning for every child.

Her passion centres around the belief that when teaching is relevant and engaging and the focus is upon sustained investment in our educators, then everyone can be successful in mathematics.

INTRODUCTION: CREATING MATHEMATICIANS

The purpose of this book is to inspire and support you, the teacher, to use rich and open activities that bring mathematics to life in your classroom. Each chapter presents tried and loved practical tasks that engage and motivate young learners. Using the ideas in this book to enhance mathematics teaching will help you to develop confident and resilient learners of mathematics, who relish challenge and believe in themselves as users and makers of mathematics. At the heart of the activities in this book is the view that mathematics develops thinking and reasoning skills valuable in all aspects of life. In modern society, where the ubiquity of digital technologies means the answers to factual questions and numerical calculations are readily available, being able to interrogate the veracity of the information obtained and to think and reason mathematically is far more important than being able to recall facts or calculate using a formal algorithm.

In a climate of educational reform and change, new curricula, government-promoted educational ideologies and higher expectations of attainment, perceived best practices and priorities in primary mathematics can appear to be shifting constantly. Yet primary teachers remain committed to developing mathematicians through rich learning experiences despite the external environment. By focusing on understanding key mathematical concepts and the connections between them, the priorities in mathematics teaching are clear, whatever the policy landscape. This introductory chapter discusses both the ethos of creating mathematicians and the priorities, in terms of the challenges in moving beyond whole number, for primary mathematics. Within each section, a number of actions are proposed that can be readily incorporated into your practice.

NURTURE A MATHEMATICIAN'S MINDSET

Mathematics is an inherently abstract subject - it happens in the head. It is unique in the curriculum, as it is inherently conceptual. This makes it challenging both to teach and to learn. Children who have regular opportunities to surprise themselves believe they can achieve and develop a mathematician's mindset. Learners' attitudes towards mathematics have a remarkable influence on their success. When teachers believe in each child's capacity to learn mathematics, every child will believe in themselves as learners and as mathematicians. This positive mindset, when shared and celebrated, is a vital ingredient for a successful classroom. Teachers must champion a love of mathematics and promote a growth mindset (Dweck, 2006) to help children develop a positive and enquiring disposition towards mathematics.

A common misconception is that some people are naturally good at mathematics – there is absolutely no evidence to support this notion despite its popularity in Western culture. In other cultures, the expectation is that all children can learn mathematics well, and they have the opportunity and support to do so.

- Call the children in your class mathematicians.
- Celebrate every child's engagement with mathematics.
- Praise children's effort and process, not outcome.
- Reassure children that they may not understand yet but they will.
- Use the language of 'attainment' and use it fluidly, as a child can attain at a given level on a given task on a given day, and that same child's attainment on another day at another task can be different. Avoid the language of 'ability' – as ability is an innate characteristic that cannot be changed.

Everyone is different but there should be equal opportunity for all to succeed. A popular approach in the UK classroom is to provide differentiated work so the previously lower-attaining learners are 'not overwhelmed' and previously higher-attaining learners are 'stretched and challenged'. This approach shackles children's prior attainment to their future attainment, trapping children in fixed learning trajectories (Boaler, 2015). The consequence of such an approach is that any gap in attainment is exacerbated as higher-attainers accelerate through the curriculum, having little opportunity to acquire depth of understanding, while lower-attainers are limited by a restricted curriculum that means they can never 'catch up'. In the UK, this approach has led to a wide gap in attainment between the highest- and lowest-attaining children.

In some countries (for example, Scandinavia), it is illegal to discriminate on grounds of 'ability' or prior attainment and all learners are entitled to support to enable them to access the same curriculum as their peers. In other countries (for example, Japan, China, Singapore), all children are taught together, and additional support is provided to those who have not fully grasped the lesson – the children may be identified by their teacher or self-identify. In these countries, the gap between the highest- and lowest-attainers is less extreme than in the UK. The curriculum is an entitlement for all and the teacher's responsibility is to make that curriculum accessible and engaging. In Chapter 4, Jennie Pennant provides examples of high ceiling, low threshold tasks that are both extendable and accessible to all children.

PROVIDE OPPORTUNITIES TO EXPLORE PATTERNS, RELATIONSHIPS AND STRUCTURES

Mathematics is concerned with pattern, relationships and structure. By encouraging learners to notice patterns and relationships and drawing learners' attention to the inherent structural relationships, they will develop a rich interconnected understanding of mathematics that will provide firm foundations for future learning. Although much of primary school mathematics is concerned with developing children's computational skills, by focusing on developing children's ability to reason about mathematical patterns, structure and relationships and to use mathematics to solve problems, we can promote depth of mathematical understanding.

- When learning multiplication facts, provide opportunities to explore and understand how these facts are related, for example:

  o $3 \times 4 = 4 \times 3 = 3 + 3 + 3 + 3 = 4 + 4 + 4$ (drawing on the commutative law of multiplication and additive properties of multiplication)

  o If you know $3 \times 4 = 12$ then you also know $4 \times 3 = 12$; $12 \div 3 = 4$; $12 \div 4 = 3$

  o using doubling, halving, and multiplying and dividing by powers of ten, many other results can be quickly deduced, for example: $24 = 6 \times 4 = 3 \times 8$; $30 \times 40 = 1200$; $300 = 120 \div 0.4$, (applying multiplicative reasoning)

  o if you know one result, you can deduce another: $13 \times 17 = 221$ so $14 \times 17 = 221 + 17$ (drawing on additive properties of multiplication).

- Provide opportunities for children to create, extend and explain their own shape and number patterns.

MATHEMATICAL THINKING

Children learn best in safe learning environments where mistakes are welcomed; they are challenged to think and reason, and given opportunities to explain their thinking. Making mental mathematics central to mathematics learning develops mathematical thinking. Mental methods should always be the first resort, with manipulatives and jottings used as aids for thinking.

- Ask all children to think about how they would complete a calculation 'in the head' and then share their different approaches.

  o Ask 'How do you work out 18×5?' Give children time to think on their own, then time to explain their thinking to a partner and then share with the whole class.

  o The answers reveal their mathematical thinking and develop their mathematical reasoning skills, for example, the distributive law: $10 \times 5 + 8 \times 5$, $20 \times 5 - 2 \times 5$; halving and doubling 9×10, $18 \times 10 \div 2$.

  o Pictorial representations of answers using arrays to support understanding.

Encouraging learners to consider how they might tackle a task and then discuss with their neighbour or in a small group before actually tackling the task can help to develop 'thinking before doing' as a *modus operandi*.

SUPPORT LEARNING THROUGH EFFECTIVE USE OF MANIPULATIVES AND MODELS

Mathematical understanding is best developed through rich practical experience (after Bruner's theory that children go through three developmental stages of learning: iconic, enactive and abstract). This includes using manipulatives and models to support children's mathematical understanding, or making jottings or drawing pictures to support their mental work. These can help children to clarify their thinking, develop their reasoning and articulate their approach to problem solving. Children's understanding of fundamental notions in mathematics, such as place value and geometric properties, are best supported with the use of manipulatives. The use of manipulatives and informal methods are equally valuable for older children as they are for young children. Alison Borthwick explores the use of manipulatives in mathematics learning and Ruth James focuses on the use of outdoor resources in Chapters 2 and 3 respectively. All learners benefit from exploring the many ways that mathematical concepts can be represented. It helps them to develop their own personal mathematical models and to appreciate how similar structures can emerge in very different situations.

- Exploit different relationships between numbers by ordering numbers on a number line or hundred square.
- Apply different understandings of the properties of shape by drawing polygons using Logo, dynamic geometry software, geometric equipment: a pair of compasses and a straight edge, or on a co-ordinate grid.
- Represent place value using a variety of manipulatives, for example, Dienes (base ten) equipment, place value tokens and place value arrow cards.

UNDERSTAND SYMBOLS

Mathematics is a truly global language - the symbols and syntax are used all around the world. Alongside the development of conceptual understanding, children need to learn about the use of symbols, for example, knowing the equals signs means the expressions on either side are the same. If children only ever see a calculation followed by = they will struggle to record missing number problems or identify equivalent calculations. In recent research (Jones et al., 2013) about children's understanding of the equals sign, the most surprising outcome was that children could not complete the equation: $7=\square$. The most common wrong answer was eight. From a young age, children need to understand what symbols mean. In some teaching schemes, children begin their work on number by comparing and ordering so they meet less than (<) and greater than (>) at the same time as, or even before, equals. This helps children to understand equality as a special kind of comparison. Children who understand the relationship between equality and inequality will know that if $a > b$ then there is some c such that $a = b + c$ and $a - c = b$. The emphasis here is on recognizing and expressing generality, as opposed to using letters to represent numbers *per se*.

- Discuss the equation: $7 = \square$.
- Introduce 'less than (<)' and 'greater than (>)' at the same time as, or even before, 'equals (=)'.
- Provide opportunities for children to explore relationships between inequality and equality such as if $a > b$ then there is some c such that $a = b + c$ and $a - c = b$.

PROMOTE TALK FOR REASONING

Social constructivists believe that children construct their own meanings through interactions with others. Discussion in the classroom about mathematics is vital to children's learning. Children need to be able to communicate their ideas accurately and increasingly succinctly. This relies on being able to use mathematical vocabulary as part of everyday communication. Children acquire a great deal of language through normal interactions both in school and beyond, but to fully understand the way vocabulary is used in mathematics, they need to be given the opportunity to explore and use it in lessons.

- How many different ways can you speak in words $9 + 5$?
- I'm thinking of a polygon with four sides and at least one right angle. What shape might it be?
- Halving is the same as dividing by two, which is the same as multiplying by a half.

The latter is an example of a statement that children can be invited to discuss and decide whether it is always, sometimes or never true. Such statements challenge children to experiment with examples, check carefully and construct arguments to justify their conclusion. They can expose children's partial understandings and help them appreciate mathematical relationships.

One way to focus on the development of conceptual understanding is to teach mathematics in the medium of a modern foreign language. This is known as the Content and Language Integrated Learning (CLIL) approach, exemplified by Pauline Palmer and Sarah Lister in Chapter 9. Providing a meaningful context in which to develop the modern foreign language, benefits learning of both the language and the mathematical concepts. Similarly, when working with learners for whom English is an additional language, support from articulate peers or an adult can help to support conceptual understanding and articulation of reasoning about mathematics. Discussing mathematics in their home language can be helpful for some learners.

CONTEXTUALIZE LEARNING

A common dilemma in teaching mathematics is whether to instil competence in 'the basics' and then teach how to use those skills in solving problems or whether competence and problem solving can be developed together. In contextualizing learning opportunities by developing basic competence and problem solving together:

- learners have more opportunities to see purpose and make connections, becoming more motivated to become 'competent' in 'the basics'

- learners can appreciate how mathematical techniques are tools for solving problems

- learners gain a deeper conceptual understanding.

Richard Skemp (1976) introduced the notion of 'instrumental' and 'relational' understanding. Instrumental understanding means that learners could perform mathematical techniques competently. Relational understanding means that learners had connected understandings of how and why the techniques worked. Children need to have both instrumental and relational understanding – there are times when it is really helpful for learners to go into 'automatic', for example, being able to quickly recall a number fact or the meaning of a mathematical word. By understanding the concepts that underpin these facts and words, learners are more likely to be able to use a variety of mathematical procedures (instrumental understanding) flexibly in a variety of contexts (relational understanding). When we, as teachers, embrace this idea of 'variation' teaching, both in terms of variation in procedures and variation of contexts, we are better placed to consolidate children's instrumental and relational understanding.

- Encourage children to develop their own strategies for finding the area of different shapes, for example, triangle, parallelogram, trapezium.

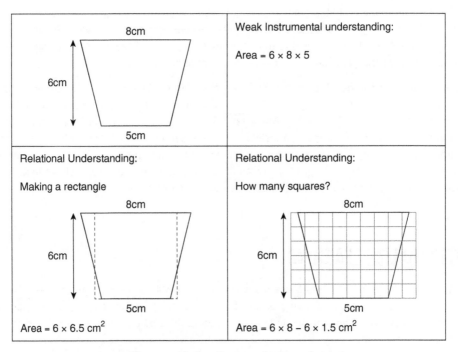

Figure 1   Finding the area of a trapezium

Asked to find the area of a trapezium, a child who thinks finding area involves multiplying two numbers that define a rectangle with the required area or finding the number of unit squares that fit inside the shape, as opposed to multiplying numbers together, is more likely to be successful.

The Dutch RME (Realistic (or Realizable) Mathematics Education) approach encourages working on mathematics in contexts that make sense to learners and nurturing the development of intuitive and informal understandings of mathematics. RME is a systematic programme of mathematics curriculum development involving teachers and researchers working together. The empty number line (ENL) as a model for recording calculations comes from RME.

- Use number lines throughout children's early experience of number to locate numbers, appreciate neighbours, identify missing numbers and reorder when numbers are 'muddled' on a number line.

These experiences are followed by counting in steps forwards and backwards, recognizing when number combinations are easier or harder, building to a powerful conceptual image that can be used to support informal calculation (see Figure 2).

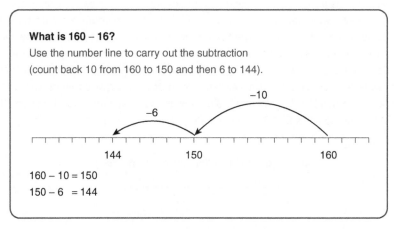

What is 160 – 16?
Use the number line to carry out the subtraction
(count back 10 from 160 to 150 and then 6 to 144).

$160 - 10 = 150$
$150 - 6 = 144$

Figure 2   Example of using a number line

- Encourage children to use diagrams and pictures to support their reasoning when solving problems; this is a powerful approach for all primary age groups.

A tank of water with 171 litres of water is divided into three containers, A, B and C.

Container B has three times as much water as container A.

Container C has $\frac{1}{4}$ as much water as container B.

How much water is there in container B?

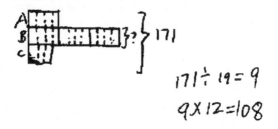

Figure 3   *Example of using diagrams and pictures when problem solving*

Source: question and child's solution (Fong and Lee, 2005)

DEVELOP MULTIPLICATIVE REASONING BY EXPLORING PROPORTIONAL RELATIONSHIPS

Multiplicative reasoning is particularly challenging for many learners. Research (Nunes et al., 2009) suggests that multiplicative reasoning is not a natural progression from additive reasoning but something that needs to be developed in parallel. In the Early Years where children talk about 'how many, more or less', they will also begin to say 'I need four times as much' (if four children are going to do the same task) and consider 'fair shares' (when sharing a bag of sweets). Working on how many times bigger or smaller as well as how much bigger or smaller can help to develop these different ways of thinking. For older children, a double number line can help children when working with proportional relationships, for example: 'If 250g of cheese costs £3.00 what does 100g cost?'

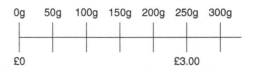

Figure 4   *Example of using a double number line*

- Discuss proportional relationships when working with shapes. Recognizing shapes that only differ in size (for example, squares, circles, regular polygons) and names that define a whole host of different shapes (for example, rectangles, triangles, quadrilaterals, polygons) is an important aspect of developing the idea of proportional relationships.

- Provide opportunities for children to use and explore double number lines when working with proportional relationships.
- As children become familiar with number bonds to ten, deepen their understanding by adding multiples of 100 to 1000, or multiples of 1000 to 10 000, for example: $3 + 7 = 10$; $300 + 700 = 1000$; $3000 + 7000 = 10\,000$

CONNECT THE FOUR OPERATIONS, EXPLICITLY

It is commonplace to refer to the 'four operations' as though they are distinct. For learners, the more they appreciate the connections between operations, the more secure their understanding and confident flexibility when tackling calculation. Addition and subtraction are 'inverse' operations - that is they 'undo' one another, for example: $4 + 5 = 9$ is 'undone' by $9 - 5 = 4$. Perhaps more importantly, all subtractions can be replaced by the addition of a negative number, that is: $9 + -5 = 4$. Similarly, multiplication can be thought of as repeated addition; and division, the inverse operation of multiplication, can be thought of as multiplication by the reciprocal, or repeated subtraction, for example: $3 \times 4 = 12$ is shorthand for $4 + 4 + 4$ and can be undone by $12 \div 4 = \frac{12}{4} = 12 \times \frac{1}{4} = 12 - 4 - 4 - 4$. Of course, division becomes much more complicated when it is not exact - how do you interpret the remainder? $14 \div 4$ can be undone in two distinct ways: $3 \times 4 + 2$ or 3.5×4.

- Regularly explore and discuss the relationships between operations to reinforce children's understanding of their connectedness. This will help children to apply operations to solve problems and appreciate that there is no ambiguity in expressions such as: $5 + 3 \times 4$ or $5 - 4 + 1$. Replacing the multiplication and subtraction with addition makes the answer clear: $5 + 4 + 4 + 4$ and $5 + - 4 + 1$. Brackets are used when the order of operations needs to be altered, for example: $(5 + 3) \times 4$ or $5 - (4 + 1)$.

MOVING BEYOND WHOLE NUMBERS – THE CHALLENGE OF MEASURES

ROUNDING

One of the most challenging steps for learners is when they move from counting and working with whole numbers to measuring. Measuring necessitates the use of approximation and numbers in between the whole numbers. This can be challenging for learners confident that $1 + 1 = 2$, which is always true for whole numbers. When dealing with measures, children who have deep understanding realize that it is possible that $1 + 1$ is anything between one and three depending on the accuracy of the measure. The measure of one to the nearest whole number defines an interval from 0.5 up to, but not including, 1.5, so when two such measures are added together the answer lies in an interval from one up to, but not including three. However, should those two measures of one total more than 2.5 they will be 'rounded' to three. This is conceptually challenging but within the grasp of some children.

> • Provide opportunities for children to explore the effects of rounding, for example, the range of possible areas of a rectangle with sides of 5cm and 10cm.

FRACTIONS AND DECIMALS

The numbers between whole numbers cause further consternation as they can be written in many ways, unlike the whole numbers where there is a unique symbolic representation for each number. At first we might meet halves and quarters – but even these present a challenge since two quarters is the same as one half. It is perhaps no surprise that the earliest systematic use of fractions by the Egyptians 5000 years ago was restricted to unit fractions (where one is the numerator or top number) and doubling these unit fractions required complex tables to ensure they were written as a sum of unit fractions, for example: $2 \times \frac{1}{3} = \frac{1}{2} + \frac{1}{6}$. The Egyptian conception of fractions was not the same as ours. Children also need to recognize the use of decimals to represent the numbers that are between whole numbers. This is an extension of the base ten place value system.

> • Use Dienes (base ten) equipment to explore the relationship between adjacent places. Ten of these makes one of those, for example: 'ten ones' make 'one ten' ($10 \times 1 = 10$), 'ten hundredths' make 'one tenth' ($10 \times 0.01 = 0.1$ or $10 \times \frac{1}{100} = \frac{1}{10}$). This is a particularly powerful way of understanding and representing place value.

Understanding decimals as a shorthand for fractions that have powers of ten as the denominator (or bottom number) is vital, if children are to be able to work confidently in situations where they need to deal with numbers that are not whole numbers. The use of a place value system is not new. About the same time as the Egyptians, the Babylonians were working with base 60 and could represent numbers using powers of 60 that extended both to the very large and the very small. In Chapter 12, Sue Pope's exploration of the historical roots of mathematics includes an activity exploring ancient number systems.

TIME

Time is probably one of the most challenging measures that children have to grasp in their primary years: the seemingly arbitrary naming of days of the week and months of the year, and the analogue clock with its 12 points for hours, when there are actually 24 hours in a day. Those 12 points are also used for minutes, but there are 60 minutes in an hour, so each point is worth five minutes.

> • There are at least two hands: the minute hand moving twelve times faster than the hour hand. If there is a second hand, how many times faster does the second hand move? Using geared clocks when teaching time can help children to appreciate how both hands move, albeit at different speeds.
> • Ordering events, matching clock faces to events and regularly drawing children's attention to the time throughout the day can all help children to learn to tell the time. Like reading, it is well worth getting parents and carers to help too.

If the greatest number used for hours is 12 then a.m. or p.m. need to be used, whereas if the greatest number used is 23 then nothing further is added so 'half past ten' in the evening can be written as 10:30 p.m., or 22:30, or even 2230. There are discussions to be had about what happens after 23:59 - and why it is 00:00 and not 24:00. A further challenge is the digital clock. A common misconception with reading digital clocks is to think there are 100 minutes in an hour. Digital clocks that use a colon between the hours and minutes should be used to help avoid this. A colon draws attention to the fact that you are not working in base ten.

- Use the clock face when working on multiples of five, fractions and angles.

TEMPERATURE

Another challenging measure is temperature. Temperature is quite unlike other measures in the sense that when making comparisons it cannot be twice as hot or cold, whereas something can be twice as long or have three times the mass as something else. In our day-to-day experience we will come across temperatures that are below freezing; colloquially these are spoken as 'minus' but in the classroom we refer to numbers less than zero as 'negative'. Minus has the potential for confusion with subtraction, whereas negative makes it clear that it is about the location of the number on the number line.

AREA

Area is the first compound measure that children meet. The concept of the space enclosed by a 2D boundary is challenging to explain and understand.

- Estimate areas by counting unit squares. Explore questions like, which type of leaf has the greatest area?
- Compare the area of right and left hands to help reinforce the idea about the 2D space within a boundary being measured in square units.
- Make explicit the relationship between the area of a rectangle and multiplication of two numbers.

VOLUME/CAPACITY

Another compound measure that children will meet in primary school is volume/capacity. The volume of something is the three-dimensional space that it occupies - only containers have capacity (in other words, the maximum volume that containers can hold). Volume of solids is measured in cube units and children can explore the volume of cuboids with linking centi-cubes. Children are likely to be familiar with volume of liquids and capacity of containers measured in litres, centilitres and millilitres long before they meet volume of solids in cube units. One of the great joys of metric units is that a volume of 1cm^3 holds 1ml, so a cube of side 10cm has a capacity of one litre.

ANGLE

Angle is a measure of turn. While colloquially we might say, 'Go right 100m', in mathematics a turn happens at a point, whether opening a door or a book or turning an object – the point at which the turn occurs does not move. A common misconception about angle size is illustrated in Figure 5:

Figure 5   *Example of a misconception about angle size*

- Children need practical experiences of folding and investigating angles. Under what conditions does a fold bisect (that is, exactly halve) an angle?
- Use programmable robots to explore right, left and turns of different magnitude.

For primary school children angles are measured in degrees and there are 360° in a full turn. The first measure of angle that children learn is the right angle. We are surrounded by right angles at every corner of every page and many other places. What is a left angle? Although there is no such thing, if all our illustrations of right-angled triangles have the triangle in the same orientation, children may assume there might be a left-angled triangle. Humans have a tremendous capacity to spot patterns and generalize; it is how we make sense of our world.

- Draw attention both to 'what something is' and 'what it is not' to support children's understanding and to help them draw conclusions by considering the whole picture.

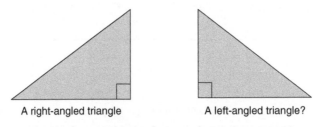

A right-angled triangle   A left-angled triangle?

Figure 6   *Is there such a thing as a left-angled triangle?*

The equipment used for measuring angles can pose particular challenges for learners. The semi-circular protractor with its double scale and the gap between the straight side and the scale make it very difficult to use, and it does not support conceptual understanding. An angle measurer helps consolidate conceptual understanding – a single zero and a knob to turn at the centre reinforces the idea of angle as a measure of turn that happens at a point.

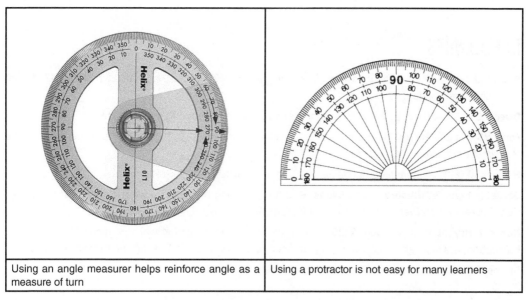

| Using an angle measurer helps reinforce angle as a measure of turn | Using a protractor is not easy for many learners |

Figure 7   Angle measurer vs. protractor

BRINGING MATHEMATICS TO LIFE IN THE CLASSROOM

Creating a positive learning environment in which children believe in themselves as learners of mathematics, excited by the challenge and eager to work with others to discover more, requires teaching that is subordinate to learning. The chapters in this book are full of activities that introduce learners to rich opportunities, making connections with other areas of mathematics, other aspects of the curriculum and life beyond. They exploit children's imagination, creativity and empathy to enrich the learning experience and nurture their mathematical development. See in particular, Chapter 8 by Karen Wilding, Chapter 10 by Diana Cobden and Chapter 11 by Tony Cotton and Helen Toft for exciting ideas about how to use everyday contexts, art and drama, respectively, for developing mathematical understanding.

Parents and carers are children's primary educators – see Chapter 13 by Josh Lury for creative ideas to enhance mathematics learning at home. Learning mathematics should be an enjoyable experience: in Chapter 1, Maria McCardle and Abigail Gosling show how even with the youngest learners, play can stimulate mathematics learning; Ray Huntley in Chapter 7 describes games that can be easily adapted for a variety of learners and topics, and which encourage discussion and reasoning; in Chapter 5, Cherri Moseley uses stories as an engaging context for learning; and in Chapter 6, Pablo Mayorga shows how digital technologies can enrich learning. Finally in Chapter 14, Mike Ollerton draws on his extensive experience to offer activities that can support children preparing to move on to secondary school.

The most important thing for children to learn in mathematics in the primary years is how to learn mathematics (Haylock, 2010: 12). Making changes to classroom practice is often easier and more likely to be successful when teachers work together, identifying priorities for development and agreeing strategies to achieve goals. We encourage you to share the ideas in this book with colleagues and develop collaborative approaches to incorporating rich activities into your mathematics curriculum.

REFERENCES

Boaler, J (2015) *The Elephant in the Classroom. Helping Children Learn and Love Maths.* (2nd edn) Souvenir Press: London.

Dweck, C (2006) *Mindset: The New Psychology of Success.* New York: Random House.

Fong, NS and Lee, K (2005) 'How primary five pupils use the model method to solve word problems', *The Mathematics Educator,* 9(1): 60-83.

Haylock, D (2010) *Mathematics Explained for Primary Teachers.* London: Sage.

Jones, I, Inglis, M, Gilmore, C and **Evans, R** (2013) 'Teaching the substitutive conception of the equals sign', *Research in Mathematics Education,* 15(1): 34-49.

Nunes, T, Bryant, P and **Watson, A** (2008) '*Key understandings in mathematics learning*', Oxford: Nuffield Foundation. Available at: http://www.nuffieldfoundation.org/key-understandings-mathematics-learning.

Skemp, RR (1976) 'Relational understanding and instrumental understanding', *Mathematics Teaching 77,* 20-26.

FURTHER READING

Gifford, S (2005) *Teaching Mathematics 3-5: Developing Learning in the Foundation Stage.* Buckingham: Open University Press.

Griffiths, R, Gifford, S and **Back, J** (2016) *Making Numbers: Using Manipulatives to Teach Arithmetic.* Buckingham: Oxford University Press.

Hopkins, C, Pope, S and **Pepperell, S** (2004) *Understanding Primary Mathematics.* London: David Fulton.

Ryan, J and **Williams, J** (2007) *Children's Mathematics 4-15: Learning from Errors and Misconceptions.* Buckingham: Open University Press.

1

MATHEMATICS THROUGH EXPLORATION AND PLAY

ABIGAIL GOSLING AND MARIA MCARDLE

── IN THIS CHAPTER ──

This chapter:

- helps you to understand the importance of play in learning
- explores definitions of 'play'
- prompts you to think about the different types of play
- considers the mathematical learning environment
- supports the development of children's logical thinking through role play.

We start from the premise that young children are meaning makers, problem solvers and pattern seekers from birth, and that they live their lives in a world that is rich with mathematical potential. From these first-hand experiences they garner spontaneous everyday mathematical ideas that lay the foundations for scholarly and scientific concepts (Vygotsky, 1987; Van Oers, 2001). Play and exploration have a central role in supporting young children's growing understandings of mathematics, and through engaging in imaginative play, children are able to bridge the gap between their innate and culturally embedded experiences towards the realm of mathematics that they will encounter as they continue their journey through school.

We need to remember that very young children learn differently to older primary children. For example, too rigid and linear an approach to children's learning of early number concepts and operations could dictate that Early Years provision might have specific, separate sets of resources, on the assumption that children will pass through distinct stages in their mathematical understanding. A more flexible approach allows children to select resources and develop their own strategies, with the teacher 'scaffolding' learning, and introducing new objects, materials and concepts. The child develops a repertoire of approaches, as well as the self-regulatory abilities that enable them to develop as an autonomous learner. With the advent of two-year-old and nursery provision in school settings, it will become increasingly important that teachers provide very different experiences in Early Years classes than they would for older children. While being encouraged to continue to learn through playful activities, so they notice mathematical concepts, the tenor of the activities for older children will necessarily be more structured.

Often, however, we confine play (in general and) in mathematics to the Early Years and children, parents, teachers and carers assume it is something to be grown out of (Pound and Lee, 2011). If children are not allowed to play, explore and discover the awe, wonder and beauty of mathematics, they could be turned off it, possibly for life.

WHAT IS PLAY?

For young children in the Foundation Stage, play is the medium through which most of their learning will take place, for a very good reason. Vygotsky points out:

> *In play, the child is always behaving beyond his age, above his usual everyday behaviour; in play he is, as it were, a head above himself. Play contains in a concentrated form, as in the focus of a magnifying glass, all developmental tendencies; it is as if the child tries to jump above his usual level.*

> (Vygotsky, 1978)

Play is an exceedingly complex phenomenon that combines into a single whole, very different strands of thought and experience, helping the child to create abstract thought. It is the medium by which links between different aspects of learning embedded in a maturing brain, become established (Robinson, 2008). Play is something the child chooses to do: the child decides how to play, how long to sustain it, what the play is about and who to play with. It engages their bodies, minds and emotions. For very young children it is an essential part of the learning process and needs to be fully understood, and valued, by teachers, carers and parents.

Key characteristics of play in its many forms are:

- *it is highly creative, enabling young children to engage in possibility thinking (Craft, 2002)*

- *it is open-ended and imaginative, including thinking beyond boundaries and challenging themselves (Vygotsky, 1978)*

- *it requires active engagement, a key aspect of how young children learn (Robinson, 2008)*

- *it is deeply satisfying. Learning should be a positive experience that adds to our self-esteem and wellbeing (Roberts, 2006).*

(DCSF, 2009a)

There are many different forms of play. For example, construction play can involve spatial and mathematical knowledge, problem solving and reasoning in particular, but mathematical learning can take place in less obvious play types. Children involved in socio-dramatic play in the home corner, mixing ingredients when making cakes involves estimation and measuring; exploratory play in the sandpit or water tray using different containers involves exploration of volume and capacity; locomotor play such as climbing trees involves children in estimation of space and position. It is more a matter of us, as adults, 'seeing' the mathematical learning that is going on in children's play. We need to put on our mathematical glasses (see Figures 1.1, 1.2 and 1.3)!

Figure 1.1   Exploratory play

Figure 1.2   Outdoor exploration

Figure 1.3   Catie mixing

REFLECTION

Consider Figures 1.4, 1.5 and 1.6 and think about the mathematical learning going on. What mathematical ideas are the children exploring?

It is through play that children begin to develop mathematical understanding as they explore, make and communicate their personal meanings. This is often referred to as 'symbolic play' since children use actions, speech or resources (for example, natural resources, unit blocks) as symbols or signs to mean something specific. Often, between the ages of three and four years, children begin to attach mathematical meanings to some of their marks and representations, using their marks as symbols to think about quantities and numerals. Children use their own symbols in flexible ways: this helps them understand that written symbols can be used to carry different meanings for different purposes (DCSF, 2009b).

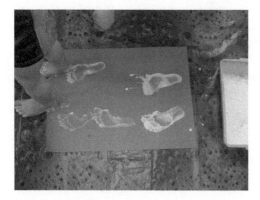
Figure 1.4   Foot painting

Figure 1.5   Mirror pyramid

Figure 1.6   Outdoor role play

Worthington and Carruthers (2006) suggest that mark making should occur spontaneously. DCSF (2008) agrees, stating that all too often, mark making is used to record after children have finished a practical activity and that children are taught to use symbols but not to apply them to practical situations.

The Williams Review (2008) made clear that effective Early Years mathematical pedagogy is built on play, and that it is important to make the most of everyday routines and spontaneous learning to develop mathematical skills and concepts. Play is at the heart of the curriculum for the Early Years; the Early Years Foundation Stage Statutory Guidance states:

> *Each area of learning and development must be implemented through planned, purposeful play and through a mix of adult-led and child-initiated activity. Play is essential for children's development, building their confidence as they learn to explore, to think about problems, and relate to others.*

> (DfE, 2017)

Although this makes clear that there needs to be a balance between adult-led and child-initiated learning, it is not advocating discrete teaching sessions focusing on mathematical learning. Circle time or table-top activities are not key activities – it is much better to weave mathematical activities throughout the day to support an 'ongoing culture of mathematical enquiry' (Carruthers and Worthington, 2011). The adult-led sessions are just that – adults may introduce a specific task or resource to initiate the children's learning with a clear mathematical learning objective in mind but the children are given independence and autonomy to play and develop their mathematical understanding. Emphasis in the Early Years classroom is on child-initiated activity, with the adult-led sessions contributing and feeding the children's self-directed experiences. It is not always easy to see the difference between the two, with many practitioners describing adult-led activities as child-initiated, but if we consider these suggestions on what play is, it becomes clearer:

> ***Adult-led activities*** *are those which adults initiate. Although the activities are not play, they should be playful – with activities presented to children that are as open-ended as possible, with elements of imagination and active exploration that will increase interest and motivation for children. As well as focused activities with groups of children, adult-led activities can include greeting times, story times and tidy-up times.*

> (DCSF, 2009a)

Child-initiated activities have many characteristics in common with play. They may involve play of many types, or they may be seen by the child as an activity with a serious purpose to explore a project or express an idea which the child may not see as purely play.

(DCSF, 2009a)

Children also need to be given extended periods of time in which to engage with mathematical experiences, in order to reflect upon and refine their mathematical understanding. We want children who can reason. We need to allow them to notice, to explore patterns, to make connections and for this, they need time to not only play but also time to reflect on their play.

As early as 1926, Wallas and later, Gallate et al. (2012), defined four stages of creativity and suggested that in being creative, we have to be given time to consciously reflect on a task, *knowing that we will come back to it* (incubation stage), so that we can get to a problem-solving stage (verification).

If exploratory play is linked to problem solving, what about imaginative play? Imagination enables us to visualize (Clements, 2014); therefore, in order to move between Bruner's (1966) enactive, iconic and symbolic stages of cognitive development, exploratory play is necessary. Sylva et al. (1976) and Devlin (2000) make links between children's imaginative play and their ability to conjecture, which Mason et al. (2010) argues is needed to problem solve.

Are we born to be problem solvers, as stated in the introduction to this chapter? González et al. (2005) discuss our funds of knowledge, and Pound and Lee (2011) cite that our ability to problem solve depends on the experiences and strategies that we have developed. So, to make mathematics real, do we need to use our imaginations? Cremin et al. (2015) discuss the importance of teachers being creative and in valuing creative ideas in themselves and children; hence children need teachers' permission to be creative. Moyles (1989) and Bruner (1986) demonstrate that playing (what Bruner terms the enactive mode) and Moyle's spiral play allow new learning to constantly occur in familiar contexts.

This may mean a radical rethink of the routines and expectations of staff in the school/setting and not only in the Early Years setting. The practice needs to be characterized by an ethos for mathematical learning that values 'creative, flexible thought and which promotes approaches which will give lifelong support to thinking mathematically' (Pound, 2006). The vision and values of the adults in the classroom with regard to play and learning are crucial to this, and often this needs to be explicitly discussed and agreed upon.

Children are not developmentally ready to sit still and listen to an adult teach them in a didactic fashion for long periods of time. Expecting children to sit still for the number of minutes that corresponds to their age in years is a helpful adage. Young children are inherently active beings and through play they can become actively engaged in learning about mathematics through hands-on experiences that correspond to their current interests.

As young children enter the nursery or reception class, we do not always know about their prior learning experiences, or what, as discussed above, González et al. (2005) call the children's 'funds of knowledge'. Play offers the children embedded uses of mathematics imitated or adapted from experiences they have had at home that will help us to ascertain what they do know. Playful learning is open-ended and places few limitations on young children's thinking, allowing us to tune in to their understanding and knowledge. By offering them the opportunity to learn from their play, we give them the best possible chance of developing positive dispositions and attitudes towards mathematical learning. Play also offers children the opportunity to challenge their own thinking, to follow their own lines of enquiry, to create their own form of mathematical graphics and reflect on what they are doing in a meaningful context.

Drama can enable children to explore language and ideas (see Kpelle game later in this chapter). If we consider play as allowing children (and adults) the opportunity to explore mathematics in a safe way, in a way 'above their heads' (see earlier in this chapter), giving them opportunities to discuss and shape their learning, such as during role play, for example, opticians, supermarkets, markets, etc., then we are introducing real-life opportunities that involve 'real' mathematics.

THE MATHEMATICAL LEARNING ENVIRONMENT

Teachers cannot really 'plan' children's play, because this would be against the choice and control that are central features of play. Teachers can plan *for* children's play by creating high-quality learning environments and ensuring that children are allowed time to develop their play (DCSF, 2009a). The provision in the early years, and we would argue, throughout primary education, both inside and outside, needs to offer a potentiating environment (Claxton and Carr, 2004), a provocation for mathematical development, maximizing each child's potential through the richness, breadth and robustness of their possible engagement with it. Children should be encouraged to be persistent and curious thinkers through questioning and collaborating with the resources, each other and the adults supporting them in order to develop in flexibility and sophistication in their thinking.

The environment can be seen as the third educator, with resources and experiences that can invite the children to explore and examine a variety of mathematical ideas quite naturally as part of their play (Edwards et al., 1998). It is important for children to access the resources independently; we can be confident in their ability to gain mathematical learning from the resources if we have chosen the resources wisely. Indeed, the entire environment is adult-constructed and led for the child to initiate their response, so it really is important to reflect very carefully upon what we are providing, and how we organize it. Young children do not need an abundance of resources, rather they benefit from carefully selected open-ended real-life materials that they can use in their play in imaginative and symbolic ways. Here are some examples.

HOME CORNER

If we take the home corner as an example, this is a staple part of the early years classroom and can offer many opportunities for playful mathematical learning.

The home corner should be stocked with a few carefully chosen real pots and pans, cutlery, plates, etc. of different size and mass. Large amounts of plastic plates, cups, saucers, pans, etc. will simply not give the child the opportunity to experience at first hand the concepts of mass, size, capacity, volume in quite the same way. Indeed, plastic crockery and cutlery, plastic food, etc. often end up as a muddle stuffed in the plastic washing machine – displaying a schematic behaviour rather than contributing to mathematical, or any other, type of learning.

Calendars, timers, clocks and watches can be used to help children to become familiar with time.

Writing pads, pencils, etc. should be available for children to represent their early graphical mark making.

Dressing-up clothes of different sizes, especially footwear, can offer lots of opportunities to experience volume and capacity.

FOREST SCHOOL

The Forest School/area within an Early Years and primary setting can provide rich and creative opportunities for exploring mathematical concepts outdoors. There are countless opportunities to explore shape, space and measure, with opportunities and space to notice, be creative, inspire awe and wonder and be involved in 'real-life' mathematics, rather than 'Mathsland' mathematics (Boaler, 2009).

Figure 1.7   Home corner cooking area

Most writing on Forest Schools focuses on the Early Years but if we look at the *Learning Outside the Classroom Manifesto*, it states: 'We believe that **every** young person should experience the world beyond the classroom as an essential part of learning and personal development, whatever their age, ability or circumstances' DfE (2006). How many children (and adults) fail to be energized by going outdoors, where they have opportunities to see patterns, make connections, and to notice?

Consider collecting twigs, stones, leaves, seeds, and flower heads – looking for and at patterns, sorting and classifying, and counting. Look at symmetry – reflective and rotational. You could introduce Phi – the golden ratio of 1.618 : 1 (approx.). When flower seeds grow in spirals, they grow in this ratio. Measurements of various parts of the human body have the same relationship. Great works of art are painted in this ratio. Mathematics is about illuminating relationships such as those found in shape and nature (Boaler, 2009).

Figure 1.8   Finding wooden poles to build a tipi

Figure 1.9   Using similar-length poles for the tipi

Figure 1.10   Cutting triangles out of material for the tipi

Use bricks for tessellation and even rotate and reflect leaves, and try some Escher-esque creations that tessellate (see Figure 1.11).

Scavenger/treasure hunts are an ideal way for children to explore position and movement. Older children could create trails for younger children or more challenging trails for children in neighbouring classes. These could lead to buried treasure or involve mazes (either natural or man-made).

Build tipi, for which you will need about five to seven similar-length poles. This in itself allows for a wealth of vocabulary to be explored. Can you find similar lengths of wood? Are those shorter/longer? Which poles are the shortest/longest?

Figure 1.11   Using bricks and leaves for tessellation

Cut triangles out of scrap material and sew or glue together to form a covering that can be wrapped around the structure. How many triangles are needed? What size do they need to be?

Knight (2011) likens heuristic play to 'trial and error' learning. During a recent activity with student teachers, we investigated spells and potions. We collected herbs, mixed them, scaled up and down the quantities of each and noticed the effect that it had on taste, smell and appearance.

OUTSIDE THE CLASSROOM

Learning outside the box – that is, the classroom box, taps into children's natural curiosity, whether it is in the outdoor area, in the school hall, corridors or outside the school grounds. Children can make more noise, be messier and do things 'bigger' than they can in the classroom, while still working in a familiar environment, although often being allowed to notice it for the first time.

Children can use and build with boxes, thereby exploring their spatial awareness – what child does not try to cram themselves into an enclosed space? How big would the space need to be to fit one child, five children, ten children, or all of the children?

Children can see and make 2D nets; then try to visualize the 3D version.

Ball games can be played to reinforce counting rhymes.

In this way, providing real-life, meaningful and contextualized resources is essential for very young children, as it is for all children. We need to immerse children in a mathematics-rich environment; we tend to do this very naturally for literacy but may be less confident or less aware of the need to do this for mathematics. If children have these experiences in the Early and Primary Years, it is argued that they will be able to move more easily between abstract concepts (Bruner, 1966).

THE ROLE OF ADULTS

For all children in the Primary Years, the role of the adult is crucial. It is here that teachers, carers and parents need to 'see' the mathematical learning opportunities in children's experiences; it is about putting on your 'mathematical glasses' and perceiving the potential of classroom activities. It is worth conducting an audit of all the mathematical provision, experiences and routines you offer in the setting and linking them to the curriculum learning outcomes (for a useful online audit tool, see EYQISP, 2011). Sharing the outcomes with staff, carers and parents can raise awareness of mathematical learning.

The importance of high-quality interaction, where adults are participant observers and use dialogic questioning to scaffold the understanding of mathematical concepts for children is of paramount importance. We need to tune in to children to understand, support and extend their mathematical learning:

Practitioners must consider the individual needs, interests, and stage of development of each child in their care, and must use this information to plan a challenging and enjoyable experience for each child in all of the areas of learning and development.

(DfE, 2017)

It is essential that we actively listen and engage in shared, sustained conversations to clarify, challenge and extend children's mathematical learning. Here the role of the adult is important: knowing the children well, understanding their prior experiences and levels of mathematical development really helps to support future learning.

Teachers also need to model mathematical language and behaviour in the classroom and use appropriate mathematical terminology modified to suit the children's stage of development. Children as young as three relish 'big' words: if they are introduced to them in the context of meaningful, playful activities, they will understand what they mean as they have first-hand experience of them and then naturally incorporate them into their vocabulary.

We must not forget the importance of involving parents and carers in their children's learning. Not only can we learn a great deal from parents and carers about the children's experience of mathematics at home, but we can also support the parents and carers to build on what the children learn at school. Take-home activities should not just be about practising skills but should also promote a more holistic and playful approach to 'homework'. Resource boxes that include a relevant story with mathematical content (see Chapter 5 for more ideas on this), suggestions for number-spotting in the environment and a digital camera to record the experiences can be created to encourage parental involvement.

The following activities could be adapted for older/younger children and resources replaced with others to suit your own setting.

ACTIVITY

Pattern making and weaving

Introduction

Many schools have railings or fencing of some kind. This can be a perfect resource for experimenting with pattern making and weaving and, in so doing, for introducing concepts of sequence (copy, continue, create), repetition and ordering. It allows children to create and notice pattern on a large scale. These experiences form the basis for further mathematical exploration.

Resources

- if fencing or railings are not readily available, orange plastic safety netting, trellis work, plant netting, etc. are suitable alternatives
- long strips of different colours and textures of materials, for example, ribbon, string, wool, strips of materials, scarves, ties
- a variety of objects that can be threaded on to the strips (beads, twigs, toilet rolls, leaves)
- digital cameras to photograph patterns.

Key vocabulary

- in, out, up, down, across, in front, behind, top, bottom, diagonal, (possibly introduce left and right).

Useful links

- http://www.childrens-mathematics.net/references_worthcarruth.htm
- http://www.childrens-mathematics.net/taxonomy.pdf

Setting the scene

Teachers can encourage children to experiment with pattern by reading stories that have patterns as an element of the narrative. David McKee's *Elmer* might be an interesting starting point. Alternatively, looking at embellished material or sari hangings can be a very tactile starting point to introduce and inspire young children's interests.

Trigger questions

- Tell me about your pattern.
- What do you particularly like about it? Why?
- What is the same and what is different?
- What do want to add next? Why?

Review and reflect

Have all children had the opportunity to experience this activity?

Use the photographs to help the children revisit their pattern making. What do you want to draw the children's attention to? How might you link this to the environment, art, architecture, etc?

Share the experience with parents/carers so they can encourage children to notice pattern in the home and local environment, for example, tiles in the bathroom, patterns on buildings and pavements, patterns on clothing, etc.

Encourage parents to bring in 'wow' moments (see Figure 1.12) to add to the children's learning journals.

Figure 1.12   Example of a 'wow' moment: a child's 'special pattern' (brought into school by her parent) made from shells collected at the seaside

ACTIVITY

Role play

According to Dienes (1963), children begin to abstract through their participation in games. The need to explore is not confined to children. 'The research scientist in his laboratory and the child engaged in exploratory play have more in common than either has with most school children working for examinations' (Skemp, 1989). Skemp further advocates that there should be a more playful approach to the learning of mathematics.

Ernest (1986) argues that games are an effective vehicle for teaching mathematics. Should it be 'learning' mathematics or 'discovering' mathematics? You often hear enthusiastic children saying, "we didn't do any maths, we just played games". In playing games, you cannot merely rely on rote learning; there are too many variables coming into play in the turn-taking, decisions that other players make, etc.

Introduction to a role-playing game

The Kpelle of Africa have a riddle involving a man, a boat, a goat, cassava leaves and a leopard. The man needs to transport all of the items across the river but can take only one item across at a time. He cannot leave the leopard with the goat or it will eat it. He cannot leave the cassava leaves with the goat or the goat will eat the leaves. This logical game uses mental skill.

Figure 1.13   Kpelle riddle

Resources

- children to take on the roles of the man, goat, leopard
- leaves
- large box or container to represent the boat (for example, playground equipment). A plastic hoop could be used to represent the boat for the people to travel in
- digital cameras to photograph scenarios.

Setting the scene

Children work in small groups to try to solve the riddle by acting it. Goat bleats with delight if it is left alone with the leaves and tries to eat them. The leopard pounces if it is left alone with the goat.

Encourage children to mark make/jot as they work.

Trigger questions (once several possibilities have been explored)

- Tell me about the possibilities you have tried?

- How could you record your attempts?

- Does the man have to come back with an empty boat?

- Could you make up your own problem with characters from a book that you have been reading in school? Take for example, *The Gruffalo* by Julia Donaldson, in which a mouse, fox and owl go on an adventure and the Gruffalo has to help them to climb a tree, one at a time; or J.K. Rowling's *Fantastic Beasts and Where to Find Them* from the world of Harry Potter. Replace the man, goat, leopard and cassava leaves with a troll, centaur, unicorn and pixie.

Review and reflect

Have all children had the opportunity to experience this activity? Do you need to allocate roles to ensure that everyone has an active part?

Use the photographs to help the children revisit their logic problem. What do you want to draw the children's attention to?

Encourage the children to develop further logic game scenarios (possible homework task).

Eliot (1999) discusses play in which young children engage in ways of reflecting on, storing and retrieving their experiences. With play, are children 'messing about' or are they testing boundaries? Are they finding out what is safe and what is not? What has serious consequences and what has not? By drawing out the mathematics in play and in providing a rich environment in which we are ourselves are prepared to play, we can help to make mathematics real and enjoyable for all.

REFERENCES

Boaler, J (2009) *The Elephant in the Classroom*. London: Souvenir Press Ltd.

Bruner, JS (1966) *Toward a Theory of Instruction*, Cambridge, Mass.: Harvard University Press.

Bruner, J, Jolly, A and **Sylva, K** (1976) *Play: Its Role in Development and Evolution*. New York: Penguin.

Carruthers, E and **Worthington, M** (2006) *Children's Mathematics: Making Marks, Making Meaning.* (2nd edn) London: Paul Chapman Publishing.

Carruthers, E and **Worthington, M** (2011) *Understanding Children's Mathematical Graphics: Beginnings in Play*. Maidenhead: Open University Press.

Claxton, **G** and **Carr**, **M** (2004) 'A framework for teaching learning: learning dispositions', *Early Years International Journal of Research and Development*, 24(1): 87–97.

Clements, **DH** and **Sarama**, **J** (2014) *Learning and Teaching Early Math*. New York: Routledge.

Craft, **A** (2002) *Creativity and Early Years Education*. London: Continuum.

Cremin, **T**, **Reedy**, **D**, **Bearne**, **E**, **Dombey**, **H** and **Burnett**, **C** (2015) *Teaching English Creatively: Learning to Teach in the Primary School*. 2nd edn. Abingdon: Routledge.

DCSF (2008) *Practice Guidance for the Early Years Foundation Stage*. Available at: https://webarchive.nationalarchives.gov.uk/20130321061316/https://www.education.gov.uk/publications/eOrderingDownload/DCSF-00266-2008.pdf.

DCSF (2009a) *Playing, Learning and Interacting*. DCSF: Nottingham.

DCSF (2009b) *Children Thinking Mathematically: PSRN Essential Knowledge for Early Years Practitioners*. DCSF: Nottingham.

Devlin, **K** (2000) *The Maths Gene: Why Everyone Has It, But Most People Can't Use It: Why Everyone Has It, But Most People Don't Use It*. New York: Basic Books.

DfE (Department for Education) (2006) *Learning Outside the Classroom: Manifesto*. Available at: http://www.lotc.org.uk/wp-content/uploads/2011/03/G1.-LOtC-Manifesto.pdf (accessed: 24 September 2016).

DfE (Department for Education) (2017) *Statutory Framework for the Early Years Foundation Stage*. Available at: https://www.foundationyears.org.uk/eyfs-statutory-framework (accessed 24 July 2016).

Dienes, **Z** (1963) *An Experimental Study of Mathematics Learning*. London: Hutchison.

Edwards, **C**, **Gandini**, **L** and **Forman**, **G** (1998) *The Hundred Languages of Children*. 2nd edn. Greenwich/London: Ablex Publishing.

Eliot, **L** (1999) *What's Going On in There? How the Brain and Mind Develop in the First Five Years*. New York: Bantam Books.

Ernest, **P** (1986) 'Games. A Rationale for Their Use of the Teaching of Mathematics in School', *Mathematics in School*, 15(1): 2–5.

EYQSP (Early Years Quality Improvement Support Programme). 2011, http://www.foundationyears.org.uk/wp-content/uploads/2011/10/EY_Quality_Improvement_Support_Programme (EYQISP).pdf)

Gallate, **J**, **Grant**, **A** and **Grant**, **G** (2012) *Who Killed Creativity? And How Do We Get It Back?* Australia: Wiley & Sons Ltd.

González, **N**, **Moll**, **L,** and **Amanti**, **C** (2005) *Funds of Knowledge: Theorizing Practices in Households, Communities, and Classrooms*. New Jersey: Lawrence Erlbaum Associates.

Knight, **S** (2011) *Risk and Adventure in Early Years Outdoor Play – Learning from Forest Schools*. London: Sage.

Mason, **J**, **Burton**, **L** and **Stacey**, **K** (2010) *Thinking Mathematically*. (2nd edn). Harlow: Prentice Hall.

Moyles, **J** (1989) *Just Playing? The Role and Status of Play in Early Childhood*, Buckingham: Open University Press.

Pound, **L** (2006) Supporting Mathematical Development in the Early Years. Maidenhead: Open University Press.

Pound, **L** and **Lee**, **T** (2011) *Teaching Mathematics Creatively*. Routledge: Oxon.

Roberts, **R** (2006) *Self-Esteem and Early Learning: Key People from Birth to School*. London: Paul Chapman Publishing.

Robinson, **M** (2008) *Child Development from Birth to Eight*. Maidenhead: Open University Press.

Skemp, **RR** (1989) *Mathematics in the Primary School*. London: Routledge.

Van Oers, **B** (2001) 'Educational forms of initiation in mathematical culture', *Educational Studies in Mathematics, 46*: 59-85.

Vygotsky, **LS** (1978) *Mind in Society: The Development of Higher Psychological Processes*. Cambridge, Mass.: Harvard University Press.

Vygotsky, **LS** (1987) 'Thinking and speech', tr. N Minick, in RW Rieber and AS Carton (eds), *The Collected Works of L.S. Vygotsky: Vol. 1. Problems of General Psychology* (pp. 39-285). New York: Plenum Press. (1st edn 1934).

Wallas, **G** (2014) *The Art of Thought*. London: Solis Press. (1st edn, 1926).

Watson, **A** and **Mason**, **J** (2006) *Mathematics as a Constructive Activity: Learners Generating Examples*. New Jersey: Lawrence Erlbaum/Taylor and Francis.

Williams, **P** DCSF (2008) *Independent Review of Mathematics Teaching in Early Years Settings and Primary Schools*, Final Report. Nottingham: DCSF.

2

USING MANIPULATIVES IN THE MATHEMATICS CLASSROOM

ALISON BORTHWICK

— **IN THIS CHAPTER** —

This chapter:

- shows you what is meant by 'manipulatives'
- helps you to understand the importance of manipulatives in the learning and teaching of primary mathematics
- features many activities that show you how to use manipulatives effectively to enhance and support children's learning of mathematics.

Manipulatives (also referred to as representations or mathematical models) are key mathematical resources needed to support the teaching and learning of mathematics. They are physical constructs that can be used to embody, illustrate and demonstrate some of the most important mathematical ideas. If learners are to become mathematical, they need to acquire mathematical knowledge, develop a range of mathematical skills and understand key mathematical concepts. Many researchers (for example, Krutestskii, 1976; Carpenter et al, 1999; Goldin and Shteingold, 2001) have all highlighted the importance of using representations (of which manipulatives are part) to support the learning of mathematics.

Manipulatives help learners to develop a conceptual understanding of what they are learning. While we can use visual (pictorial) representations, this chapter is going to focus on those resources that can be physically manipulated by both adults and learners.

WHY ARE MANIPULATIVES IMPORTANT?

Mathematical understanding centres on learners first having concrete, practical experiences before it becomes an abstract subject in which they need an understanding of symbols and how they are connected. The way in which teachers represent mathematical ideas and processes has a great impact on how well learners learn. It is important for learners to use concrete materials in order for them to be able to think about and understand the mathematics, rather than just acquire it without sufficient understanding.

The relationship between concrete, pictorial and symbolic (abstract) representations of mathematics is often complex. Learners can sometimes think that mathematics is based on tricks rather than actually understanding the mathematical concepts. Manipulatives provide an essential dimension to learners' understanding of these concepts. The aim for learners is that they use manipulatives during their mathematical learning experiences from a concrete to a pictorial to an abstract understanding of mathematics. Learners do not learn mathematical knowledge through being told facts that they have to memorize. They construct mathematical knowledge through exploring, discovering, researching and using. Manipulatives demonstrate the move from physical representations of mathematics to using mental images and finally to more abstract mathematics. However, while this may appear to be seen as a linear progression, it is not. While learners may move away from using manipulatives as they become more experienced and familiar with mathematical concepts, there is always a role for manipulatives at all stages of learning. One of the strengths in using manipulatives is that they can provide other ways of seeing and understanding the mathematics, as illustrated by the examples in this chapter.

Although a few learners may progress automatically to abstract methods, most learners (of all ages) need lots of experience in using practical resources. It is the difference between understanding mathematics or simply doing without understanding. Manipulatives not only allow learners to represent their thinking with concrete materials, but they also assist learners in forming useful mental pictures to support memory and reasoning.

HOW CAN WE USE MANIPULATIVES?

A teacher's ability to use manipulatives is a key aspect of how well learners will learn. Teachers need to consider what it is they want learners to learn and which mathematical resource is the best to support this. It is not always obvious what each piece of equipment is for. Even when it is easy to see what it is for, you may not know how to use it to help learners learn. The manipulatives described in this chapter outline which mathematical concepts each resource supports. For example, resources such as beads and counters lend themselves to supporting counting-based strategies, while place value charts are designed to show the relationships between multiplying and dividing by ten and 100.

Using manipulatives will not guarantee mathematical understanding. Teachers need to show learners why a resource is a mathematical model and how it supports mathematical understanding. Manipulatives have different strengths and limitations. While some learners may favour one model over another, it is important to use a range and variety when teaching mathematics. Furthermore, different manipulatives emphasize different aspects of a mathematical concept. As Kaput (1992) highlights, learners need to experience a range of manipulatives so they can develop and build up knowledge towards some of the complex mathematical ideas they will meet.

While having access to a range of manipulatives is important, there are other components that we must also consider. The variety and range of manipulatives we use can support learners' reasoning about the mathematical insights afforded by different manipulatives (Borthwick and Cross, 2018). Encouraging learners to reason will help them to articulate and see the connections between different representations. Barmby et al. (2009) advocate a problem-solving approach to mathematics, rather than a separate strand or idea. If learners see all mathematics as a problem to solve, including the use of manipulatives, they will be much better placed to apply their knowledge in unfamiliar situations and engage with novel tasks.

This chapter will focus on the following manipulatives:

- beads and counters

- Numicon

- number tracks and number lines

- hundred squares, ten squares, one squares

- linking cubes

- Dienes blocks

- place value charts and cards

- Cuisenaire coloured rods.

Each section outlines which mathematical areas the manipulative represents. Classroom activities are included within these sections with further activities at the end of each section. Manipulatives are not restricted to an age or phase of learning. They can and should be used by all learners of mathematics. The amount of time in a lesson will vary. Some learners may use the manipulatives all lesson, while other learners may move between using a concrete resource, pictorial representations and working in the head. However, moving between concrete, pictorial, abstract (Bruner's enactive, iconic, symbolic) is not time limited or fixed in one direction. Learners should feel able to move freely between different representations and then back to concrete should they need this to support their understanding. Staying with the 'realizable' context is an essential part of the Dutch RME (Realistic Mathematics Education) approach to mathematics. Recently I worked with some Key Stage 3 and 4 teachers whose students used coloured rods to support their algebraic thinking.

BEADS AND COUNTERS

Beads and counters are important manipulatives because they can be used to support the development of counting and calculating as well as the representation of quantity. These are essential models of mathematics for promoting a rich sense of number. Small stones, pasta shapes and buttons are a good alternative to beads.

BEADS

Figure 2.1   Beads

Beads can support mathematical concepts such as counting, representing numbers, quantity, sorting and classifying, and pattern.

ACTIVITY

Counting

- Give learners a pile of beads and ask them to count them.
- Notice if they count them individually, using one-to-one correspondence, or perhaps in groups of two or five.

Using beads for counting-based strategies also offers opportunities to combine two or more quantities, which supports early development of addition.

Using manipulatives in this way allows learners to explore the concrete, practical concept of addition before moving onto abstract number sentences.

ACTIVITY

Representing numbers

Beads also support the representation of number.

- Ask learners to show you how many two or three beads would be. Using beads to represent quantity is useful as children will begin to realize that the same numbers can be used in many contexts.
- Pick two small handfuls of beads and ask learners which pile has more beads in it.
- Now ask learners to make two piles that have the same amount of beads in them.

Beads are useful to support the development of strategies for deciding whether groups are equal, more or less.

ACTIVITY

Sorting and classifying

Beads can also be used to explore sorting and classifying activities. Ask learners to sort and classify a pile of beads according to colour, size or pattern.

ACTIVITY

Pattern

Using beads to explore pattern also encourages logical, mathematical thinking.

- Give learners a handful of beads and some string and ask them to make a bracelet. You could ask learners to make up their own patterns or give them one to follow. For example, you could say that alternate beads must be different colours, or perhaps every third bead must be red.
- Once the learners have made their bracelets, ask them to describe each other's patterns.

BEAD STRINGS

A bead string is a mathematical resource made up of ten groups of ten beads in alternate colours. The bead string supports learners in being able to describe numbers from one to 100 in a variety of ways, find their position in a sequence and talk about the composition of numbers.

Figure 2.2   Bead strings

ACTIVITY

Finding numbers through partitioning

The beads are purposefully grouped into groups of tens to support understanding of the base ten place value system. For example, finding 12 beads on a bead string shows learners that 12 can be made up from ten and two.

Ask learners to find different numbers on the bead string and explain how they found the number.

ACTIVITY

Calculating

Bead strings also support understanding of the four operations.

Asking learners to add numbers together on a bead string shows that addition is about combining quantities together. This can be performed in a variety of ways on a bead string, but it supports adding partitions of numbers that could be recorded on a number line.

Subtraction on a bead string offers two choices, depending on whether you want to find the difference between the two numbers (using a counting-up strategy) or take away.

Working out multiplication questions on a bead string illustrates the link between this operation, repeated addition, and 'skip' counting (that is, counting in groups).

(Continued)

(Continued)

Division on a bead string illustrates the grouping (but not sharing) concept, as learners work out how many groups of the divisor they can make from the dividend. This exposes the relationship between multiplication and division that can be thought of as repeated addition and repeated subtraction respectively.

ACTIVITY

Ratio and proportion

Bead strings are an excellent manipulative to support the understanding of ratio and proportion.

Ask learners to show a quarter of the bead string.

The resource is valuable for illustrating the relationship between fractions, percentages and decimals. Learners can use the whole bead string or just part of it to illustrate a quarter. Either way, they are strengthening their understanding of proportion as being part of a whole (whether the whole is represented by four beads or all 100 beads).

Ratio is a comparison of parts, and the bead string can support learners' understanding. Ask learners to show the ratio of 1:3. They might take one bead and compare it to three beads, but equally they may show ten beads and 30 beads.

COUNTERS

Figure 2.3   Counters

You can use counters to represent numbers in different ways. Like beads they can be used as counting objects. They can also be arranged in different ways to highlight number facts, particularly if you use two-sided counters.

ACTIVITY

Addition and subtraction

Counters provide a useful model for addition and subtraction facts to ten or 20. Using counters in this way shows that addition strategies have corresponding subtraction strategies. It is important to teach addition and subtraction together so that learners understand the relationships between them.

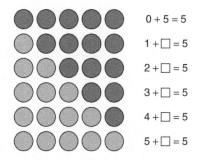

$$0 + 5 = 5$$
$$1 + \square = 5$$
$$2 + \square = 5$$
$$3 + \square = 5$$
$$4 + \square = 5$$
$$5 + \square = 5$$

Figure 2.4   Using counters for addition

Start by exploring addition and subtraction facts to five, ten and then 20. Use two different coloured counters to highlight the importance of five. Once learners are secure with the cardinal value that a group of counters represents five, they will begin to count on from five each time (instead of needing to go back to one each time).

ARRAYS, INCLUDING MULTIPLICATION AND DIVISION

An array is formed by arranging a set of objects into rows and columns. Each column must contain the same number of objects as the other columns, and each row must have the same number as the other rows.

Multiplication has certain fundamental properties that are of great importance to arithmetic, and arrays help to support this basis of knowledge. One of these is the concept of repeated addition.

Children can start from the number being multiplied (for example, the number 4 in the calculation $4 \times 3 = ?$) and add on this number in the required steps $(4 + 4 + 4 = 12)$. Using counters can support this mathematical understanding as learners can make either rows or columns of four counters three times.

Arrays also illustrate the commutative property: $3 \times 4 = 4 \times 3$. The commutative property of multiplication means that changing the order in which two numbers are multiplied does not change the product. An array with three rows of four counters has the same number of counters as an array with four rows of three counters in each row.

Arrays can be used for building multiplication facts too. It is important that children understand how multiplication facts are derived. For example, by progressively adding another column of three counters or dots, children can build the multiples of three for themselves. This representation not only assists in understanding the process, but also provides a visual image for children to draw upon as they begin to use and memorize basic number facts.

The arrays can be presented in different ways – physical objects including counters, recording dots on the page or counting squares on squared paper. The latter illustrates why an array is often referred to as the area model for multiplication. The principle is always the same but moving to a blank grid allows larger numbers to be multiplied together using convenient partitions. This powerful model provides strong foundations for progression as it readily generalizes to algebra and can be used for multiplying decimals and fractions too.

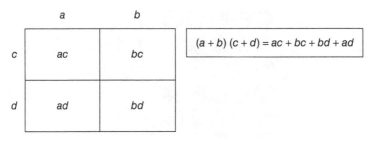

Figure 2.5   Array or area model for multiplication

The same array can be used for division (sometimes referred to as the reverse grid). $123 \div 16$ can be thought of as an array comprising rows (or columns) of 16 with a total of 123 counters; children use their multiplication facts to figure out how many groups of 16 are in 123 – seven remainder eleven: $7 \times 16 + 11 = 123$.

The same principle can be applied to odd and even numbers. An even number of counters can always be made into an array with rows (or columns) of two, but odd numbers cannot – there is always one counter left over. Making two rows (or columns) illustrates the fact that even numbers are divisible by two.

Arrays also support children's understanding of factors. When you make an array, each dimension of the array is a factor. You can ask children to explore different arrays of the same number. For example, the number 12 can be represented in three different arrays (without repeating commutative properties).

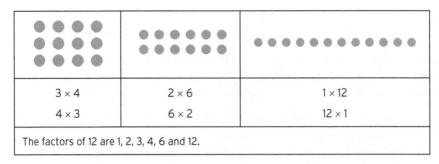

Figure 2.6   The number 12 represented in three different arrays

Exploring factors in this way will lead to the discovery that some numbers can be made into more than one array (composite numbers), some numbers can be made into square arrays (square numbers) and some numbers can only be represented by a single array of just one row (or column) (prime numbers).

SUBITIZING

Counters are also a useful model to give learners opportunities to subitize. Subitizing is the immediate recognition of a small number of objects without having to count them. Learners can subitize up to about four or five objects, more if they are arranged in particular ways (consider the arrangement of dots on dice and dominoes). This is a key skill in developing learners' ability to count as it allows learners to move away from 'counting all' and supports the development of mental calculation strategies for addition.

FURTHER ACTIVITIES FOR BEADS AND COUNTERS

- Ask learners to take a small handful of counters and estimate how many they have. Once they have estimated, ask them to check by counting them in different ways, for example, in ones, twos or threes.

- Ask learners to make patterns with counters. For example, they could make triangles or squares. If the first triangle has three counters in it, how many counters do we need for the second triangle?

- Give learners different lengths of string. Ask them to predict how many beads will fit onto their string. Once the learners have threaded their strings, count up the beads. Whose string has the most beads on it? How close are you to your estimate? Make comparisons between different strings. For example, can you find a string double in length?

- Show learners five counters. Ask them to count them so they are certain there are five. Hide the counters under a tin or piece of paper. Now ask how many counters there are under the tin or paper.

- Show me 28/56/97 beads on your bead string. Show me ten more than 35.

- Show me half of your bead string.

- What is the total of 35 + 27? Show your answer on the bead string.

- What is the product of three and four? Show your answer on the bead string.

- Draw an array on the board and ask children to work out the number it represents.

- Write a number on the board and ask children to draw an array to represent the number.

- Explore how many different arrays can be drawn for the same number, for example, 24.

- Draw an array. Ask children what multiplication sentence describes the array.

- Ask children to write story problems that describe a six-by-five array.

- Draw an array. Ask children what counting pattern is shown by your array.

- Ask children to make different arrays and work out the total number of items in each.

NUMICON

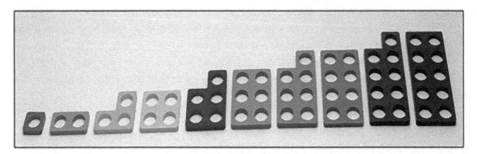

Figure 2.7   Numicon

Numicon is a valuable resource for developing early understanding of number and relationships. The spatial arrangement of the numbers 1 to 10 support the conceptual development of subitizing, number bonds to ten and odds and evens. However, Numicon is also a powerful manipulative for understanding fractions, ratio and algebra.

ACTIVITY

Hide and seek

Place tiles 1 to 10 in a bag. Using digit cards 1 to 10, turn over a card and find the matching tile in the bag – without looking!

This game helps learners to match the abstract number with a concrete representation.

ACTIVITY

Numicon towers

Ask learners to choose a tile. This is their first tower. Ask them to find other tiles that when placed on top have the equivalent value of their first tile. How high can they make their tower? Ask learners how they know they have found all the possibilities.

This activity scaffolds learners' understanding of number bonds to ten.

ACTIVITY

Fraction Numicon

Ask learners to choose two tiles and work out the proportion of the smaller one to the larger one. This task could be extended to learners creating a picture out of Numicon (for example, a house, a dog, a robot) and then working out what proportion the eyes are or the windows.

ACTIVITY

Equality

If possible, try to use some pan balance scales for this activity, which explores the concept of the equals sign in equations. Give learners an example such as $15 + 17 = x + 6$. On one side of the balance scales place the total value of $15 + 17$ in Numicon tiles and on the other side tile/s to represent 6. The scales will not balance. Ask learners what we need to add to the side with 6 in it to make the scales balance. Add in the equivalent value of 26 in Numicon tiles, thus showing that x equals 26. Ask learners to write their own linear equations and then work out the value of x using Numicon and balance scales.

FURTHER ACTIVITIES USING NUMICON

- Order Numicon tiles from 1 to 10.

- Match Numicon tiles to different piles of counters.

- Print, make playdough shapes or draw around Numicon tiles.

- If you have a Numicon base board, cover the board with Numicon tiles.

- Make repeating patterns with different tiles.

- Choose a number card and make the number using tiles in lots of different ways, to support partitioning.

- Find the missing number, by removing one of the tiles when they have been ordered from one to ten.

- Explore doubles of numbers by choosing a number (for example, 3), and then select two tiles of this number.

- Use Numicon to add, subtract, multiply and divide numbers in a concrete way.

NUMBER TRACKS AND NUMBER LINES

Number tracks and number lines are representations that allow us to show the continuous nature of numbers. They are an important image for addition and subtraction. Number tracks and number lines are often presented horizontally but they can be represented vertically too.

NUMBER TRACK

Figure 2.8 Number track

In a number track, each number occupies a cell. The numbers should start at one (not zero). Number tracks are an essential starting point for children in developing their understanding of the ordinal and cardinal value of numbers, as they aid the understanding of one-to-one correspondence between numbers and cells. Learners often enjoy jumping along a number track or placing the correct amount of objects on each number.

ACTIVITY

Missing numbers

Number tracks can be used to support the reading of numerals and locating ordered numbers.

Either draw a number track on the board or use one you already have. Miss out or cover up a number and ask children what the missing number is.

This activity supports number recognition and number sequencing.

NUMBER LINES

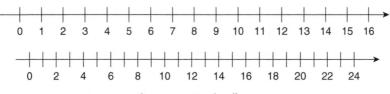

Figure 2.9   Number lines

The image of a number line begins with the concrete manipulative of the bead string, then moves to the partly imagined image of the numbered line and finally to the empty number line. In a number line, the divisions rather than the spaces are numbered. This means they can begin at any number, they can show any number sequence and ultimately, they can be expanded 'backwards' into negative numbers or scaled up to show decimal numbers and fractions. They allow the continuous nature of number to be represented and support learners counting in steps.

ACTIVITY

Pegging out the washing

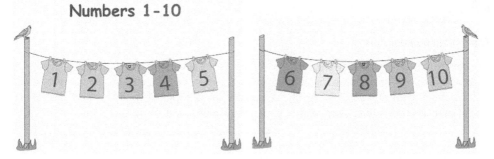

Figure 2.10   Washing line

A washing line is another version of a number line. It is important to hang the washing line at a level at which you and the learners can touch as this type of number line is ideal for learner interaction.

Ask the children to come and peg numbers onto the line in order. This could be as simple as using numbers 1 to 10, or, you could use multiples of ten from 0 to 100, or multiples of four, or decimal numbers from 0 to 1, or fractions.

Peg numbers onto the line but in a muddle. Ask children to sort out the numbers and put them back in order.

Again, this re-enforces number recognition and number sequencing.

ACTIVITY

Recognizing points on a number line

Ask children to recognize points on different number lines, using the information available.

ACTIVITY

Calculating using number lines

The use of the empty number line is a useful image for learners to keep track of their steps in mental calculation and to communicate their strategy. Both numbered and empty number lines can be used to help children complete calculations.

Give learners opportunities to use a number line to solve addition, subtraction, multiplication and division questions.

ACTIVITY

The double number line

The double number line can also be used as a model for understanding multiplication as scaling. For example, any number on the top of the number line is multiplied by 1.5 by any number below it on the bottom of the number line. The double number line is a valuable representation for converting between units, for example, cm and m, imperial and metric measures.

FURTHER ACTIVITIES FOR NUMBER TRACKS AND NUMBER LINES

- Ask children to walk along a number track, saying each number as they step onto it.

- Using a number track or line, find the numbers 6, 9, 27.

- Stand on or hide a number and challenge a friend to say what the hidden number is.

- Walk along a number track. Now stop and close your eyes. What are the next two numbers?

- Using a numbered line marked from 0 to 20, mark jumps of two along the line.

- Using a numbered line marked from 0 to 100, mark jumps of ten along the line.

- Using an empty number line, calculate 23 + 27 and 76 − 37.

HUNDRED SQUARES, TEN SQUARES, ONE SQUARES

Hundred squares, ten squares and one squares are ten-by-ten grids containing 100 numbers. Depending on the type of hundred square, they can start at 0 and finish at 99, or start at 1 and finish at 100. A ten square starts at 0.1, increases in steps of 0.1 and finishes at 10, while a one square starts at 0.01, increases in steps of 0.01 and finishes at 1. Any of the activities below can be used with any type of square.

1	2	3	4	5	6	7	8	9	10
11	12	13	14	15	16	17	18	19	20
21	22	23	24	25	26	27	28	29	30
31	32	33	34	35	36	37	38	39	40
41	42	43	44	45	46	47	48	49	50
51	52	53	54	55	56	57	58	59	60
61	62	63	64	65	66	67	68	69	70
71	72	73	74	75	76	77	78	79	80
81	82	83	84	85	86	87	88	89	90
91	92	93	94	95	96	97	98	99	100

Figure 2.11   Hundred square

Constructing the square to have increasing numbers in higher rows can be very valuable. Considering what happens when you fall off the square is also helpful, see the image overleaf.

A hundred square presents a particular image of the number system. It is a useful manipulative for counting, looking for patterns in number, addition and subtraction. On the 1 to 100 square (or 0 to 99) counting, or adding one at a time, is associated with moving horizontally across the grid. When the end of one row is reached, the count continues at the start of the next row. When counting in ones, moving down a row is adding ten.

ACTIVITY

Connecting hundred squares and number lines

When learners start to encounter and use a hundred square, help them to understand and see that it is a number track that has been cut up and reorganized into rows of ten.

160	150	140	130	120	110	100	90	80	70	60	50	40	30	20	10	0	-10	-20
159	149	139	129	119	109	99	89	79	69	59	49	39	29	19	9	-1	-11	-21
158	148	138	128	118	108	98	88	78	68	58	48	38	28	18	8	-2	-12	-22
157	147	137	127	117	107	97	87	77	67	57	47	37	27	17	7	-3	-13	-23
156	146	136	126	116	106	96	86	76	66	56	46	36	26	16	6	-4	-14	-24
155	145	135	125	115	105	95	85	75	65	55	45	35	25	15	5	-5	-15	-25
154	144	134	124	114	104	94	84	74	64	54	44	34	24	14	4	-6	-16	-26
153	143	133	123	113	103	93	83	73	63	53	43	33	23	13	3	-7	-17	-27
152	142	132	122	112	102	92	82	72	62	52	42	32	22	12	2	-8	-18	-28
151	141	131	121	111	101	91	81	71	61	51	41	31	21	11	1	-9	-19	-29
150	140	130	120	110	100	90	80	70	60	50	40	30	20	10	0	-10	-20	-30
149	139	129	119	109	99	89	79	69	59	49	39	29	19	9	-1	-11	-21	-31
148	138	128	118	108	98	88	78	68	58	48	38	28	18	8	-2	-12	-22	-32
147	137	127	117	107	97	87	77	67	57	47	37	27	17	7	-3	-13	-23	-33
146	136	126	116	106	96	86	76	66	56	46	36	26	16	6	-4	-14	-24	-34
145	135	125	115	105	95	85	75	65	55	45	35	25	15	5	-5	-15	-25	-35
144	134	124	114	104	94	84	74	64	54	44	34	24	14	4	-6	-16	-26	-36
143	133	123	113	103	93	83	73	63	53	43	33	23	13	3	-7	-17	-27	-37
142	132	122	112	102	92	82	72	62	52	42	32	22	12	2	-8	-18	-28	-38
141	131	121	111	101	91	81	71	61	51	41	31	21	11	1	-9	-19	-29	-39
140	130	120	110	100	90	80	70	60	50	40	30	20	10	0	-10	-20	-30	-40
139	129	119	109	99	89	79	69	59	49	39	29	19	9	-1	-11	-21	-31	-41
138	128	118	108	98	88	78	68	58	48	38	28	18	8	-2	-12	-22	-32	-42
137	127	117	107	97	87	77	67	57	47	37	27	17	7	-3	-13	-23	-33	-43
136	126	116	106	96	86	76	66	56	46	36	26	16	6	-4	-14	-24	-34	-44
135	125	115	105	95	85	75	65	55	45	35	25	15	5	-5	-15	-25	-35	-45
134	124	114	104	94	84	74	64	54	44	34	24	14	4	-6	-16	-26	-36	-46
133	123	113	103	93	83	73	63	53	43	33	23	13	3	-7	-17	-27	-37	-47
132	122	112	102	92	82	72	62	52	42	32	22	12	2	-8	-18	-28	-38	-48

Figure 2.12   Hundred square after Geoff Faux

Source: adapted from Geoff Faux

ACTIVITY

Exploring patterns

Hundred squares can be used to explore number patterns.

Ask the children to count in tens, starting at 6. Record the numbers on the board, for example, 6, 16, 26, 36, 46, 56 ... and then as a counting sequence as a calculation, $6 + 10 = 16$. This connects the use of the manipulative to abstract thinking and symbolic recording.

Ask learners to investigate other number patterns using the hundred square. For example, explore relationships between sets of multiples.

ACTIVITY

Calculating using hundred squares

Hundred squares are particularly useful for adding and subtracting numbers. For example, $38 + 23$ could be worked out by starting at 38, and then adding $10 + 10 + 3$ to reach 61. Similarly, $74 - 28$ can be solved by counting back first two tens then eight ones (or a vertical step of two and eight horizontal steps) to reach 46, or counting back three tens and then adding two. Another way to illustrate $74 - 28$ is to count up from 28 to 68 in tens, then from 68 to 70 in a step of two and from 70 to 74 in a step of four.

ACTIVITY

Visualization

The hundred square can be a very powerful image for exercising learners' mental imagery.

Using the hundred square, focus on the top row. Begin counting from one but stop before you reach the end. Ask learners to close their eyes and imagine the rest of the hundred square. Ask them how many more numbers there are to the end of the line. Now cover up four numbers in the hundred square. Ask learners to work out what numbers are covered.

This type of problem helps learners to understand the pattern of counting in ones or tens, using the hundred square as a visual aid.

FURTHER ACTIVITIES FOR HUNDRED SQUARES, TEN SQUARES AND ONE SQUARES

- Roll two dice. Make a two-digit (whole or decimal) number with the dice and put a counter on the hundred square to cover that number.

- Count in twos or fives on the hundred square. Ask children to see if they can spot a pattern.

- In pairs ask one child to choose a number from the hundred square. The other child has to ask questions to guess what the number could be. For example, is the number odd or even?

- Ask children to cut up a hundred square. Swap with a partner. Can you put the hundred square back together again?

- Roll three dice. Using any of the four operations and all three dice scores, make a number on the hundred square and cover it with a counter. Children can take it in turns to do this with the object of completing a chain of counters from 1 to 100.

LINKING CUBES

Figure 2.13   Linking cubes
Source: adapted from Geoff Faux

Linking cubes are a versatile resource for exploring number. Making rods of ten, where five are in one colour and five in another, is a valuable resource for exploring number bonds to ten. They can easily be used to create growing patterns, for example, multiples using simple arrays, or other growing patterns. The concrete resource provides a tool for reasoning about the number pattern generated, for example, 'the L shapes add two cubes each time – one each end of the L'.

Figure 2.14   L-shapes made from linking cubes

ACTIVITY

Exploring 3D shapes

Linking cubes are a valuable resource for exploring 3D shapes and identifying their properties including faces, vertices and edges.

Give each child five cubes and ask them to work in pairs. One child secretly makes a shape. Their partner has to make the shape with their cubes by asking yes or no questions. For example, are there at least four cubes in a line?

How many different shapes can you make using just four cubes? How can you be sure you have found them all?

DIENES BLOCKS

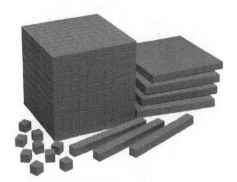

Figure 2.15   Dienes blocks

Dienes blocks are a powerful resource for illustrating base ten place value, in particular 'ten of these make one of those'. The smallest cube can be assigned any power of ten as a value, for example, 1, 10, 0.01. The resource is particularly valuable for exploring the composition of numbers and completing calculations where powers of ten are bridged, for example, 112 − 27, 86 + 27.

PLACE VALUE CHARTS AND CARDS

Place value charts and cards emphasize the idea of place value and the way numbers are constructed. They are a key model as they show the value of a digit relating to its position in a number. For example, the numbers 12, 207 and 2823 contain the digit 2, but the position of the digit 2 indicates the place value of two in each number. Place value charts and cards allow learners to see how numbers can be partitioned and recombined.

GATTEGNO PLACE VALUE CHART

Gattegno Place Value Chart

Ten thousands	10 000	20 000	30 000	40 000	50 000	60 000	70 000	80 000	90 000
thousands	1000	2000	3000	4000	5000	6000	7000	8000	9000
hundreds	100	200	300	400	500	600	700	800	900
tens	10	20	30	40	50	60	70	80	90
ones	1	2	3	4	5	6	7	8	9
tenths	0.1	0.2	0.3	0.4	0.5	0.6	0.7	0.8	0.9
hundredths	0.01	0.02	0.03	0.04	0.05	0.06	0.07	0.08	0.09
thousandths	0.001	0.002	0.003	0.004	0.005	0.006	0.007	0.008	0.009

Figure 2.16 Gattegno Place Value Chart

The Gattegno Place Value Chart consists of the numbers 1 to 9 in a row with the multiples of the other powers of ten above and below. To move between adjacent rows, you multiply or divide by ten with the digit moving to a different place. It provides the opportunity for learners to see the parallel structure of counting ones, tens, hundreds, tenths, hundredths, etc. This mathematical resource provides a cardinal image of numbers.

ACTIVITY

Additive and multiplicative place value

The place value chart helps learners to see that our number system is a place value system, where a digit does not have a numeric value until it is in a particular position. This is positional place value. The place value charts can also be used to illustrate additive place value. The number 853 can be partitioned into 800 and 50 and 3. When the individual values are added together, they give the value of the whole number. If we consider the digit 8 within the number 853, we can also determine its value by multiplying the digit by its position, so 8×100 would give us the value 800. This is the multiplicative aspect of place value.

Using place value charts allows learners to explore how numbers are partitioned and recombined for both whole numbers and decimals. This model is essential if learners are to develop different ways of partitioning numbers. For example, 64 could be split into 60 and 4, but it could also be 50 and 14 or 70 less 6. Using place value charts and cards helps learners to see the importance of place value giving them a better understanding of number structure.

ACTIVITY

Multiplying and dividing by ten and multiples of ten

Place value charts can also be used to support multiplying and dividing by powers of ten, for example, 10, 100, 0.1.

Talk with learners and discuss how the numbers in each row are found by multiplying the number below by ten. For example, $4 \times 10 = 40$, $40 \times 10 = 400$. If you skip a row, the numbers are multiplied by 100. Equally, if you go down a row, numbers are found by dividing by ten.

It is important that learners are secure about multiplying and dividing by ten, 100, etc., as it is a key mathematical skill and concept. Place value charts help learners to see that when we multiply a number by ten, the answer is ten times greater, and when we divide a number by ten, the answer is ten times less.

PLACE VALUE (ARROW) CARDS

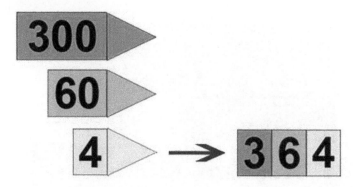

Figure 2.17 Arrow or place value cards

Place value cards (also known as arrow cards) are as useful as the place value chart and are best used alongside the chart. They are made up of sets of nine cards printed with multiples of powers of ten. The simplest sets include hundreds, tens and ones. Decimal place value cards are available too. Numbers are built by overlapping cards of different values (as illustrated above).

ACTIVITY

Partitioning

Give all learners their own set of place value cards. Ask them to put cards together to show you numbers such as 56, 108, 399, etc. Now give learners numbers (for example, 24, 528) but ask them to write down the partitions (for example, 24 = 20 + 4).

FURTHER ACTIVITIES FOR PLACE VALUE CHARTS AND CARDS

- Point to numbers on a place value chart and ask the class to say them out loud.
- Cover three numbers on the place value chart. Ask learners to write down on mini-whiteboards the three-digit number that is hidden.
- Say a number and ask learners to make it using place value cards.
- Show me a number that is between 4.9 and 5.
- Point to 3 tenths, 7 hundredths, 5 thousandths.
- Describe what is happening when we multiply 1.25 by 100.
- Describe the mathematical process to get from 300 to 3.

CUISENAIRE COLOURED RODS

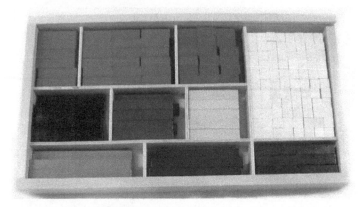

Figure 2.18   Cuisenaire rods

Coloured rods are sets of different-length rods, designed to develop an understanding of mathematical relationships. They can be used to represent number and have the flexibility to be assigned any number you choose. They are a powerful manipulative for conceptual understanding of mathematics including calculations, fractions, ratio and algebra.

Learners should use letters to record their work with rods, for example, w + w = r, w < r,

---

ACTIVITY

Comparing lengths

Ask learners to sort, order and compare the lengths of different rods. They may choose to do this with all ten rods or just a few of them. Notice how they compare and reason between the different lengths. Which one is the longest? Shortest? How much longer is the orange rod compared to the red rod? Encourage them to compare rods and combinations of rods using the language of less than, equal, greater than, then using the symbols <, =, >.

ACTIVITY

Generating relationships

Trains are made by putting rods end to end. If the same rods are used, then multiples and fractions naturally follow. w + w = r means that red is twice as long as white, and white is half the red.

Introduce learners to formal recording of these relationships, for example, $w = \frac{1}{2} \times r$; $r = 2 \times w$. How many relationships like this can they find?

ACTIVITY

Number bonds

One use of the rods is to assign a value to each rod. So, the shortest rod (white) is given a value of one and the longest rod (orange) is given a value of ten. In this way rods can support the development and understanding of number bonds.

Ask learners to show you all the different combinations where one set of rods placed together is equivalent to ten. Encourage them to work systematically starting with two rods and then using more than two rods.

The rods can be assigned different values. What if the smallest length of rod is given a value of, for example, 10, 15, 0.1, 100. What would the value of each of the other rods be? Learners can now use the rods to develop other number relationships.

ACTIVITY

Calculating with rods

Coloured rods can support thinking when working out calculation problems. For example, when working out the sum of 24 and 13, learners can use two rods to represent the numbers 24 and 13, and a third rod (placed underneath the first two) to represent the answer. Used in this way the manipulative is emphasizing the understanding between a part, part, whole relationship. While the coloured rods do not provide the answer, they are an important manipulative in helping learners to understand the mathematical processes involved in thinking about and understanding the calculation.

The coloured rods can be used in this way to support subtraction, multiplication and division questions as well as missing number questions. Sometimes one or all of the parts could be missing, but in other questions it could be the whole that is missing.

ACTIVITY

Linear equations

Coloured rods can be used algebraically because the rods can be used to represent any number. In the equation $x + 3 = 9$, we have two parts and a whole. One rod can represent the whole (9) and then two rods can be placed either above or below the whole, to show that two parts are needed. As above, the coloured rods do not give learners the answer, but they do support understanding, as opposed to solving an equation through tricks.

FURTHER ACTIVITIES FOR COLOURED RODS

- If the smallest rod is worth five, what value are the other rods?

- How many different ways can you connect the yellow, light green and red rods together?

- Use the rods to illustrate this problem: If Hannah earns £2.50 an hour, and she worked seven hours, how much did she earn altogether?

- What fraction of the orange rod is the yellow rod?

- Use the coloured rods to show this linear equation: $3x = 12$.

CONCLUSION

Learners of every age benefit from the use of manipulatives. A mathematically rich environment will have attractive stimulating mathematical displays and a wide variety of manipulatives. Children should be able to select the resource they want to use when working on mathematics. However, children will only select a resource if they are familiar with it. This means it is important that you model the use of different manipulatives and offer challenging experiences that exploit and reveal the inherent structure within the resource, mindful of its limitations.

REFERENCES

Barmby, **P**, **Bilsborough**, **L**, **Harries**, **T** and **Higgins**, **S** (2009) *Primary Mathematics: Teaching for Understanding*. Maidenhead: Open University Press.

Borthwick, A and **Cross, A** (2018) *Reasons to Reason in Primary Maths and Science*. London: Sage.

Carpenter, **TP**, **Fennema**, **E**, **Franke**, **ML**, **Levi**, **L** and **Empson**, **SB** (1999) *Children's Mathematics: Cognitively Guided Instruction*. Portsmouth, NH: Heinemann.

Goldin, GA and **Shteingold, N** (2001) 'Systems of representation and the development of mathematical concepts', in AA Cuoco and FR Curcio (eds), *The Roles of Representation in School Mathematics* (2001 Yearbook of the National Council of Teachers of Mathematics). Reston, VA: National Council of Teachers of Mathematics, pp 1–23.

Kaput, **J** (1992) 'Technology and mathematics education', in DA Grouws (ed.), *Handbook of Research on Mathematics Teaching and Learning*. New York: NCTM, pp. 515–50.

Krutetskii, **V** (1976) *The Psychology of Mathematical Abilities in School Children*. Chicago: University of Chicago Press.

FURTHER READING

Delaney, **K** (2010) 'Making connections: teachers, and children using resources effectively', in I Thompson (ed.), *Issues in Numeracy in Primary Schools*. Milton Keynes: Open University Press.

Griffiths, R, Gifford, S and **Back, J** (2016) *Making numbers: using manipulatives to teach arithmetic*. Oxford: Oxford University Press.

Houssart, J (2000) 'The role of number resources in the daily mathematics lesson', in T Rowland (ed.), *Proceedings in the British Society for Research into Learning Mathematics*, 20 (3): 37–42.

3
MATHEMATICS OUT AND ABOUT

RUTH JAMES

---- IN THIS CHAPTER ----

This chapter:

- explores why mathematics out and about matters
- helps you to look again at the spaces available to you for learning and teaching mathematics
- supports your use of 'big' resources to support learning
- features logic puzzles where the children can take on the role of characters and 'act out' the problem.

WHY SHOULD WE TEACH MATHEMATICS OUTSIDE OR AWAY FROM THE CLASSROOM?

Children can make more noise, more mess and physically move at a greater speed outside. The outside environment often has uneven ground or slopes and differing surfaces including concrete and grass that help to accentuate the difference between indoors and outdoors. Children manage their own risks outdoors, from changes in temperature to changes in climate. Outdoor learning can also include an element of heuristic learning or discovery learning through trial and improvement, encouraging resilience and promoting exploratory debate.

BIGGER SPACES MEAN LARGER SCALE

Equipment used outside can and should be on a larger scale, enabling representation of a variety of mathematical concepts in a different and often more engaging way than in the classroom, such as construction blocks or long sticks. This is likely to engage younger children in building structures or measuring spaces for a longer period of time, supporting the development of communication and reasoning skills as their design or problem-solving interaction becomes more complex.

Fresh air and an uncluttered workspace help children to focus more easily as there are different distractions than in a busy classroom. To 'inspire' means to breathe in (air) as well as to create. A larger space between children allows for use of gross motor skills to help consolidate conceptual learning before representing informally and then learning standard symbolic conventions. Outdoor learning is beneficial to children with English as an additional language as they can discover and practise ideas without the constraints and requirements of a new language.

The enjoyment of doing mathematics through outdoor learning promotes mathematical engagement by using alternative resources such as natural materials. Using sticks to make Roman numerals reinforces learning through making number representations.

Figure 3.1   Natural Roman numerals

Using stones to make arrays of numbers (Year 2 and above) is more exciting than using counters indoors. A larger space than the traditional classroom also means that children can 'be the numbers' and use each other to make number sequences, number bonds and arrays exploring how different numbers can be grouped and shared.

The use of natural materials provides an interesting link with home learning as the children's learning can be practised and repeated at home using sticks and leaves, which they have used at school without the need for specialist equipment such as Dienes or number squares. The sensory nature of using natural materials to sort by different categories to promote mathematical thinking encourages observational skills leading to scientific enquiry. However, the key here is repetition using different contexts and/or environments to nurture conceptual understanding.

Working together as a community of learners with a shared problem provides shared memorable experiences that are so important for deep learning. As well as making mathematical experiences more memorable by using the outdoor environment, they are likely to be made more meaningful by increasing engagement, which in turn helps to raise mathematical attainment. Above all, outdoor mathematics can be practical, challenging and enjoyable across all areas of the curriculum. A giant hopscotch, 1-100 square, or a number track can be used for counting, sequencing, number patterns and multiples (via skip counting).

For those children who are sensitive to bright stimuli, a natural canvas in shades of green or brown encourages concentration on the activity or task without the interference of a busy, often primary colour palette in the classroom. The open-air aspect of working outdoors lends itself to more natural sounds away from the cacophony of sound information of other children in a closer space and the interference of repetitive synthetic noise, for example, from computer programmes. Contrastingly, for whole-class teaching, a memorable rhyme sung outdoors as an aid to memory can be as loud as your neighbours will permit.

Weather should not determine whether learning is done outdoors. Children need to be appropriately dressed from sun hat and sun-cream to wet-weather and waterproof clothing following Forest School principles. Children also need to be aware of safety when moving and carrying larger equipment, which is where your expertise of knowing the cohort of children as well as knowing the outdoor space is vital. There should be a standard school risk assessment for children working in outside spaces, and it is important that you consider all elements carefully.

A TOOLKIT FOR OUTDOOR MATHEMATICS

Outdoor mathematics requires a permanent outdoor toolkit, designed to be used for a multitude of learning tasks and, where possible, it should be stored outside:

- cones with numbers (minimum of 1-9) or with pockets where larger numbers can be inserted

- a variety of sizes and colours of chalk

- quoits or rings that will fit over the top of the cones

- mini-whiteboards and whiteboard pens

- bibs/tabards for identification and team challenges - a set with numbers (for example, 1-30) is a really useful resource

- metre sticks and measuring tapes

- bamboo sticks of various lengths

- large and extra-large hoops

- compass point (laminated or weatherproof) cards

- a set of carpet tiles numbered 1-100, or a large ground sheet with a ten-by-ten grid marked out.

Figure 3.2   Children measure the toolkit storage box

ASSESSMENT AND RECORDING

Outdoor recording needs to be considered carefully. Being able to make mistakes without the 'stress' of written detail allows children to try alternative ideas and take more risks with their learning than they might have otherwise done if they had to record all the information and all of their thinking on paper.

Photographs or videos are ideal for recording the activity as it is taking place and can be referred back to when in the classroom. How much 'writing up' is necessary? Children may become less enthusiastic about outdoor learning if it is always followed up with indoor writing. Digital recording can be used as the basis for assessment for learning that can be developed in future teaching. As with any teaching, you will need to decide what outcomes you are hoping children will achieve and what successful outdoor learning is likely to look like, so you know what you are looking for when recording.

NUMBER

Many mathematics curricula around the world focus on the development of number skills in primary mathematics. The national curriculum in England is no exception. Outdoor activities use and develop children's mental mathematics skills in tasks that also support the development of problem solving, reasoning and communication in a cooperative learning context.

A change of scene can be useful to reinforce specific number concepts in an enjoyable way. For example, a human number line (1–30 or 20–50) can be great fun when physical activities are involved. When all the teen numbers do some star jumps or the multiples of three stretch up their arms, children can experience the patterns in number that may be harder to appreciate on paper. For those children with special educational needs, a physical response to number properties may help their developing understanding. If this is filmed, it can be replayed to remind children and consolidate their learning.

EARLY YEARS – FINDING NUMBERS

In the Early Years, children learn to recognize numbers greater than or less than ten. Large-scale numbers can be matched to other numbers as part of a learning walk around the area to discover numbers in the environment – car registration plates, house numbers, street hydrant numbers. Children can use a digital camera to capture the numbers they find.

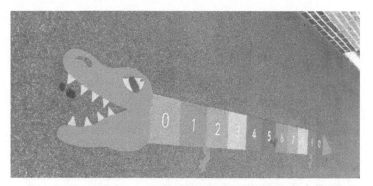

Figure 3.3   A playground number track

ACTIVITY

Finding number bonds

Give each child a number card or Numicon piece to put into their tricycle basket and then ask them to cycle to the fence or around a simple track to find the corresponding number card or Numicon piece to make the pair sum to ten. The child's choice can then be checked using the number representations on the back of the cards. Matching the Numicon pieces by fitting them together shows an array of ten.

NUMBER SQUARE

A number square is valuable for teaching and learning properties of number such as multiples, factors, primes, squares and cubes.

ACTIVITY

Number square ideas

Stand on a number that contains the digit 6, for example, then try a different digit. What do the children notice? Why does this happen?

(Continued)

(Continued)

Stand on an even number, a multiple of three, then a multiple of four. What do the children notice? Encourage them to think why this happens.

Select a number. What number is ten more, ten less, one more, one less? How would you describe the number that is one up and one left, for example?

How does the number square help you to remember number bonds to 20 (Year 1) or 100 (Year 2)?

Stand on a number. What is the nearest ten? Where can you stand if the number is nearer to 40 than 30 or 50? This experience can help to reinforce the convention that when the number ends in five, you round up not down.

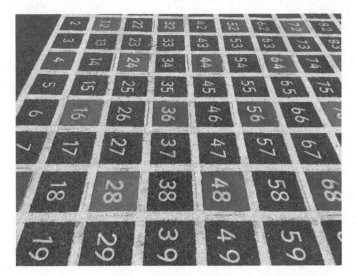

Figure 3.4   Number square

Walking or jumping on the number grid for skip counting can help to reinforce awareness of patterns in sets of multiples. Throwing bean bags into squares in response to a question provides a physical approach to developing rapid recall of number facts.

Recording using natural materials such as twigs or stones or on mini-whiteboards provides a quick assessment for the teacher. Children can extend the number square into negative and greater than 100 numbers using chalk (Year 4).

BLANK HUNDRED GRID

A blank hundred grid has a number of exciting mathematical possibilities. A permanent white-lined grid on a playground can be used as a coordinate grid, for work on fractions, decimals and percentages, and exploring different arrangements of the numbers 1 to 100.

Hundred Grid

Royal Kingston

100									
90	91	92	93	94	95	96	97	98	99
80	81	82	83	84	85	86	87	88	89
70	71	72	73	74	75	76	77	78	79
60	61	62	63	64	65	66	67	68	69
50	51	52	53	54	55	56	57	58	59
40	41	42	43	44	45	46	47	48	49
30	31	32	33	34	35	36	37	38	39
20	21	22	23	24	25	26	27	28	29
10	11	12	13	14	15	16	17	18	19
0	1	2	3	4	5	6	7	8	9

Figure 3.5 Kingston hundred grid

ACTIVITY

Unique path

Place labelled cones on the grid – the children have to work out how to get from one to another on a unique path, without overlapping or crossing.

Different sequences of labels can be used for different groups/pairs to create a set of instructions for a unique path. Children can be encouraged to think about giving instructions to a programmable robot and use turns (whole, quarter, half, three-quarters, clockwise, anticlockwise, right, left). The cones can be repositioned to provide appropriate challenge.

The extension task is to find the most efficient unique path. Recording can create a set of instructions such as 'turn left, move 1 square forward' or as a set of co-ordinates (1, 1) to (1, 3), etc.

ACTIVITY

Further activities on a blank hundred square

• Translation – moves a person/cone from one position to another describing the movements as left/right, up/down. Repeat for a group of cones/people (the object). Note that the object does not change.

(Continued)

(Continued)

- Reflection - get one group of children to arrange themselves in one half of the grid and invite another group of the same size to create a mirror image (Year 2 and above).

- Number patterns on a coordinate grid - use chalk to label the axes and then ask children to stand on the grid according to different rules: x is one, x and y are equal, the y value is one more than the x value, the y value is half the x value. What do children notice? Can they make up rules of their own?

- Invite children to stand in half of the grid, or a quarter, or a tenth. What fractions can be illustrated? For older children, half the grid can be 50 per cent or 0.5. How can you cover the greatest amount of the grid? What fraction, percentage, decimal is that?

- A blank grid can also be used to explore different ways of making a number square. The Kingston hundred grid starts with the numbers on the bottom row increasing as they go up rather than starting at the top and working down. Children could explore different arrangements using chalk or numbered carpet tiles.

- What plants/stones/insects can be found in our playground? Use metre sticks or bamboo canes 1m long to create a square. Count the different plants/stones/insects found in the square and compare with other squares. The data could be represented using natural materials as a pictogram or block graph using digital photographs.

ACTIVITY

Metre people

This is an art/mathematics activity and starts in the classroom.

Get children to work in pairs to create a representation of a person that fits on a piece of sugar paper or similarly heavy paper with dimensions of 1m by 20cm to make a one-metre person. Children can use rulers, tape measures, etc. to decide how to create their representation.

- How many heads can you get in a whole body (ratio)?
- What fraction of a person is the body, the head, the legs, etc?
- Where will the metre person's waist be?

Once the metre people have been drawn and decorated, they are ready to be used inside and outside the classroom.

Children can use the metre person to find items that are smaller or bigger than one metre; encourage them to estimate before checking. They can also look for relationships - for example, this is double/half the metre person. They can record their work with drawings or photographs.

Metre people can also be used to explore fractions of a length, for example, four metre people lined up head to toe is 4m. Half is 2m or two metre people, and $\frac{3}{4}$ of 4m is three metre people.

Metre people can also show arrays: for example, seven metre people in two rows, so there are double 7 or $7 \times 2 = 14$ metre people altogether.

Figure 3.6   Array of metre people

Another key learning point is using the language of metres to measure: for example, knowing that half a metre person is 0.5m or 50cm. Using fractions greater than one can be illustrated, for example, a height or length of 150 is 3 × 50cm or one and a half metre people.

Figure 3.7   One and a half metre people

Knowing that a metre stick is the same height as the metre person provides an experiential anchor for further work on measures: for example, imagine that you have your metre person - is this object shorter or longer than your metre person?

Taking account of the dimensions of the original rectangle, work on area, perimeter, unit conversion and decimals all become possible. For example, the 7 × 2 array has dimensions 2m for the two rows of metre people and 140cm (7 × 20cm) for the width so the area is 28 000cm^2 or 2.8m^2 - why the factor of 10 000? And the perimeter is 680cm or 6.8m - why the factor of 100?

Metre people can be used to investigate the relationship between the distance around the circle (that is, the circumference) and the diameter of the circle.

LOGIC PROBLEMS

Larger spaces are ideally suited to logic problems where trial and improvement approaches can be enacted to see 'what happens if?' and promote exploratory debate.

Using simple problems such as 'Sally lived next door to Micha but not next to Steven, and he lives three doors from Juan', gets groups of children involved physically as they take on the role of the characters in solving the problem. Recording and assessment can be carried out by the children as they check their answers to confirm the final order.

ACTIVITY

The fox, the hen and the corn problem

This activity challenges the children as to how to get the fox, the hen and the bag of corn safely across the river without the fox eating the hen or the hen eating the corn, when only one of the three can be transported in any single river crossing.

Arrange the children into small groups of three or four with a hoop for the boat and the children in each group representing either the fox, hen or bag of corn.

Challenge children to find the most efficient method for transporting the objects across the river. There are many river-crossing problems that children could research for themselves and then devise their own problem.

POSITION AND DIRECTION USING COMPASS POINTS

Compass points are important in geography (map making) and science (the movement of the Earth, for example, sunrise and sunset). Deciding where to place North, South, East and West markers in the playground and classroom helps children to appreciate their constancy. The need to describe a direction between North and West leads to North West and the other interim directions: North East, South East, South West.

ACTIVITY

Treasure hunt

Hide some treasure and prepare clues for the children in the form of a puzzle, riddle, map or similar. Older children could prepare the treasure hunt for other classes.

Small groups can take it in turns to hunt the treasure, or you could have multiple treasures so each group has something different to find.

Jump the compass

Jump to face the compass point or direction of North, East, South and West. This can then be linked to fractions of turns and angles: 'Face North, turn 180° degrees clockwise'. Children then chorus the compass point they are facing. 'Make a quarter turn anticlockwise'; 'Turn 135° degrees clockwise'; 'Turn clockwise to face North East - what angle did you turn?', etc.

DATA COLLECTION

Collecting and analysing data is an essential cross-curricular skill. Out of the classroom, children can collect data to answer questions: How do plants grow in different parts of the school grounds? How many star jumps can you complete in a minute? Does more traffic pass the school at different times of the day? How old are the trees in the school grounds? How quickly can we run around the playground? Children can count, measure, time to collect real data they can enter into a spreadsheet to analyse.

Children know that the age of a tree is found by counting the rings in the cross section, but this is not very helpful for a live tree. To estimate the age of a living tree, measure the circumference of the trunk at 1m above the ground and divide the answer by 2.5; for example, if the circumference is 122cm, the tree is about 48 years old.

A longer project of weather analysis would generate a large amount of data that could include daily rainfall, daily temperature at certain times of the day, daily wind direction (compass points again) and daily wind speed.

BIG GEOMETRY

Making 2D shapes with sticks or string allows children to use geometric properties in practical challenges. How many sticks do you need to make a regular pentagon? What shapes can you make that have only right angles?

ACTIVITY

2D shapes

Stand the children in a circle and pass a ball of string around using rules to generate shapes, for example, the first child holds the string and then passes the ball of string to the third person on their left who holds the string as well, and then passes to the third person on their left, and so on until a closed shape is created. Repeat for different rules and consider what happens and why. What rule would generate a triangle? What regular polygons can be generated in the class?

Many capacity and volume explorations involving water are best conducted outdoors. How many of this container fills that container? Children can also learn about different measures of capacity and their relationships: for example, how much bigger is a litre than a pint? How big is a gallon? They could also estimate how long it takes to fill a large a container: for example, a water butt or pond, and time it, if possible.

Visualizing 3D shapes is often a challenge for children, and outdoor experiences making large models provide a strong basis for learning. Suggested tasks allow children to make big shapes while taking risks, making mistakes, discussing and trying out ideas.

ACTIVITY

Visualizing 3D shapes

In groups, make the largest 3D shape you can with a certain number of bamboo pieces. What is the minimum number of pieces you need?

Make a 3D shape that has 12 vertices – how many different shapes can you make?

Make 3D shapes that have triangular faces only – how many different shapes can you make?

Figure 3.8   Example of outdoor equipment for exploring geometry

Figure 3.9   A hexagonal prism

For each shape children construct, they can explore the geometric properties: for example, establishing whether edges or faces are parallel, or whether faces are regular polygons. They can estimate its volume. They can distinguish between volume and surface area, and the need for different units.

MATHS TRAILS

Maths trails are a great way of helping children to notice the mathematics around them. A bank of tasks can be devised that allow teachers to put together a trail tailored for the class and the topic currently being taught. Once children have experienced a maths trail they can be challenged to devise a new task for the trail so the bank is continually refreshed. Below are some generic ideas that can be adapted and developed:

- Find shapes around the school, for example, semi-circles on the football pitch, oblongs as part of a fence.

- Identify triangles.

- Find repeating patterns.

- Find given objects using photographs taken from unusual angles.

- Find symmetrical shapes.

- Find parallel lines.

- Find right angles.

- Estimate the length of the perimeter fence.

- Use a map of the school on a coordinate grid to locate places.

- Set puzzles based on particular artefacts.

Consider other interesting questions by looking at everyday things differently, for example:

- How many rectangles are there in the window (there are more than 9)?

- Could all the children hug the school?

- How many benches are there in the school grounds? Are there enough benches for 40 per cent of the children in school to sit down?

- If you stand with your back to the front door, what is 90° or 270° to your left?

- What is at the northern-most point of the playground?

FURTHER READING AND USEFUL WEBSITES

Maths trails: www.thinkingchild.org.uk.

Early Years outdoor learning ideas by Juliet Robertson: www.creativestarlearning.co.uk.

Snails' trails activity for practical outdoor use: https://nrich.maths.org/216

Learning maths outside the classroom: www.ncetm.org.uk/resources/9268

Learning through landscapes: http://www.ltl.org.uk/

Robertson, Juliet (2014) *Dirty Teaching: A Beginner's Guide to Learning Outdoors.* Carmarthen: Independent Thinking Press.

4

MATHEMATICS FOR ALL – LOW THRESHOLD, HIGH CEILING

JENNIE PENNANT

IN THIS CHAPTER

This chapter:

- outlines what is meant by 'low threshold, high ceiling' (LTHC)
- considers how LTHC tasks fit into differentiated learning
- helps you think about the different skills that children develop when working on LTHC tasks
- shows you how to adapt activities for younger learners.

One of the challenges in the classroom is to provide activities that support the children's mathematical learning journey and enable all children to be at their learning edge throughout the lesson. Homogenous classes of children, where they are all at the exactly the same stage on their mathematical journey, are a rarity. In fact, I have never encountered one. Thus, the importance of providing a class with activities that have an easy entry point yet offer opportunities for children to stretch, deepen and extend their thinking they are vital in order to maximize the learning opportunities for all in the class throughout the week. Such activities mean that the whole class is working on the same concept and tackling the same problem, albeit at different levels of depth. We use the phrase Low Threshold, High Ceiling (LTHC) to denote such activities. The term LTHC originates in Seymour Papert's description of the central design principle of the Logo programming language (Papert, 1980). See also NRICH (2011) in Further Reading at the end of this chapter.

WHAT IS THE AIM OF LTHC TASKS?

LTHC tasks encourage children to show what they can do. They foster a very positive learning environment. Children can progress deeper and deeper into the activity as their grasp of the mathematics needed develops through the lesson, or lessons. There is no pre-conceived limit, neither is the task they are given differentiated according to their expected achievement level. They can progress through a LTHC task at their own rate. The word deeper is important here as, in a LTHC task we are looking to support the children to find patterns, look for generalizations and prove their conjectures rather than accelerate them onto a higher piece of mathematics content. The deepening process is relevant to all children, wherever they are on their mathematical journey. For example, if we think of our youngest learners, they are using this deepening process as they come to understand that three cars, three cakes, three bubbles, three clouds can all be represented by the abstract symbol 3. High Ceiling in a task enables children to dig more deeply into mathematics.

It is important to be aware that LTHC tasks develop children's process skills as well as their mathematical competence. For example, these tasks can enable children to develop their problem-solving skills, such as trial and improvement and working backwards, while using and developing understanding of mathematics, such as ordering decimal numbers. They can also develop their reasoning skills as they seek to explain their thinking: 'I'm placing 0.66 between 0.54 and 0.91 because ...'.

LTHC tasks help us to build a mathematics community at the heart of the classroom. Such a community values taking risks, 'having a go', getting 'stuck', making mistakes and the articulation and discussion of mathematical ideas. The community is a creative climate where all can engage in mathematical learning and can argue for mathematical truths. Success with a LTHC task is much more than just finding a/the solution(s). We need children to become confident with the process and the journey if they are to develop as learners and users of mathematics. We need to explicitly value the process and development of personal attributes, drawing attention to successes with any or all of these when drawing the activity to a close.

Central to this mathematics community and the use of LTHC tasks is 'maths talk' or whole-class and small-group dialogue. This helps children to share their ideas, listen to each other, build on each other's ideas and justify their thinking to others. Alexander (2010) draws attention to the fact that 'high-quality classroom interaction is one of the defining characteristics of outstanding teachers', yet we know that to enable such interaction to happen regularly and frequently in the classroom we need to explicitly model 'the talk' and support children to develop the tools they need. We need to be explicit about the development of 'talk' for all children and not leave it to the few 'verbally enthusiastic' children in the class.

RECORDING MATHEMATICAL THINKING

Finally, we need to think about how we want the children to record their mathematical thinking while engaged in a LTHC task. Undertaking one of the tasks has parallels with undertaking a piece of creative writing in English. For that we encourage the children to 'talk it, write a draft and then refine it' before we expect them to produce the final neat version. So we need to consider where and how the children can record their emergent thinking as they work on a LTHC task. They may want to make a record to help them remember what they did so that they can repeat it, or to make a record of what does not work to keep a track of what they have tried. There is no need to waste time repeating something that does not work by mistake. Such recording may well be a stepping-stone to the final solution and may look more like jottings or seem untidy. However, this recording will capture valuable mathematical thinking. We need to ensure that the children are encouraged to record this valuable thinking in their books as part of their learning journey. We need to accept that it may look less 'formal' than other work, yet it is valuable recording. It may not yet be in a form that communicates well to others. That will come later as the children's thinking reaches a conclusion that they are happy with and ready to share. A writing frame can be a useful aide to support children's communication about their work.

Before embarking on a LTHC task, consider how to nurture the community of learners and the classroom culture, and what record of the activity might be appropriate. These will contribute to securing successful children's mathematical learning. Here are three LTHC tasks, all based on grids and fluency with number. Each one exemplifies a different way in which problem solving, reasoning and the LTHC approach can be used in your classroom. Each task is easily adaptable to suit your class.

- **UNIQUE!**

    Which of these four numbers in the grid is unique and why?

    This task can be used repeatedly with the class over a number of weeks. It can be used as a starter once the children understand the way it works.

- **Awesome adding**

    Choose two numbers to add together from the grid. Which ones are easy for you and which ones are hard? Why is that?

    This task can be used to introduce problem solving and reasoning into a standard lesson on calculation.

- **Addition trios**

    How many trios can you find in this grid that are connected by addition number sentences? How do you know if you have found them all?

    This task helps children develop their problem-solving skills and uses mathematical content that is likely to be within their comfort zone.

ACTIVITY

Unique!

Resources

Each pair will need a 0–9 dice.

National curriculum and mathematical understanding links

Suitable for: Key Stage 2 (age 7–11); can be adapted for Key Stage 1 (age 5–7).

Objectives: to solve number problems using the properties of number and place value.

Mathematical understanding: properties of number and reasoning

Setting the scene

Draw a two-by-two grid on the board. Explain that that you are going to generate four two-digit numbers to place in the grid.

Throw the 0–9 dice twice to generate the first number. The first throw is the tens digit and the second throw is the ones digit. Place the number in a cell of your choice on the grid.

Throw the dice six more times to complete the grid. If you generate a number that you already have in the grid, throw the dice again to ensure that you have four different numbers. For example, your grid might be:

42	14
27	91

Figure 4.1   Example of a two-by-two grid

Invite the children to talk to a partner and decide which of the four numbers is unique.

Model the process for them by saying, 'I think that 14 is unique because it is the only one that is a teens number'. Ask them to try and think of a reason for one of the numbers to be unique that no other pair in the class will come up with (a unique reason for a unique number). This encourages them to think more deeply. Ensure they understand that there is no right answer. They simply need to be able to justify their choice of unique number with a mathematical statement.

Invite suggestions from the class. Encourage them to use the same sentence structure as you did. 'We think that xx is unique because ...'. Encourage the use of accurate mathematical vocabulary. Check that everyone understands the meaning of any new mathematical vocabulary used. For example, '27 is unique as the other three are multiples of 7'. Check that everyone knows what 'multiple' means.

Note down all their suggestions on a large flipchart. Aim for at least six different reasons. Here are some for this grid:

- 27 is unique as it is the only one that is a cube number.
- 91 is unique as all the other numbers use digits less than 8.
- 42 is unique as both its digits are even numbers.

(Continued)

(Continued)

- 42 is unique as it is the only multiple of six.

- 91 is unique as it is the only one that is divisible by 13.

You might be surprised by the pair that think laterally and say, '91 is the odd one out as the other three are house numbers in James's Street'. Check out which reasons are unique to one pair in the class, as that was the challenge set.

Support

For children who are finding it difficult to find a unique number, invite them to find two numbers on the grid that have something in common. For example:

- 42 and 14 are both even numbers.

- 27 and 91 are both odd numbers.

- 14 and 91 are both one away from a multiple of 5.

- 42 and 27 are both multiples of 3.

- 14 is a factor of 42.

Continue to re-enforce the accurate use of mathematical vocabulary.

Taking it further

Throw the dice eight times to generate a new set of four numbers in a new grid.

Invite the children to see if they can use as many of the types of reasons generated from the first grid of numbers for the second grid of numbers. Then invite them to see if they can think of any new reasons. Add these to your ongoing list of reasons that you are collecting as a class.

You can finish the activity here and return to it again another day. Refer back to your communal list of reasons and keep adding to it every time you do the activity together with the class. Which reasons get used frequently? Which reasons are harder to use? Why is that? If you prefer, you can continue further with the lesson as detailed below.

Working independently

Give each pair a 0–9 dice. Invite them to generate a two-by-two grid of numbers and devise some reasons for a number to be unique. They can also look for two numbers that have a property in common. When the children are ready, invite them to swop their grid and reasons with another pair. The new pair needs to check that they agree with the reasons given and see if they can find any further reasons to add to the list. Return the checked grid and reasons to the original pair.

Digging deeper (High Ceiling)

Looking for reasons that no other pair has thought of encourages the children to think more deeply.

In addition, you could invite them to choose four numbers for the grid that they think would make it easy to find six reasons as to why a number is unique. Ask them to list the six reasons and to explain why they chose those particular numbers.

They could also try choosing four numbers that they think makes it a hard grid and explain why they think that is the case.

As a class, over a period of weeks, you could collect easy and hard grids. Look and see what the grids have in common. This encourages the children to look for patterns, to reason and to generalize.

Wrap up

Ask the children if any pair has a new reason that makes one of their numbers unique. Check it out with the class. If everyone is happy that it is a new and valid reason, add it to the list of reasons that you are collecting as a class. Ask the children for two numbers that have something in common. Check if what they suggest is a new and valid reason. If so, add it to the list of reasons.

Figure 4.2   A two-by-two grid for a 'convince me' task

You may like to put up a grid and use a 'wrong' answer. You may like to introduce it like this, 'The Head tried this grid this morning and she says that 27 is the unique number because the others are all multiples of 6. Is she right? Convince me. If you think she is wrong how could we change the grid so that she can be right?'

Trigger questions

- What do you notice about those two numbers?
- Tell me some facts you know about each of the numbers.
- What mathematics vocabulary can you use to describe the properties of one of these numbers?
- What do you know about the factors of each of the numbers?
- What reason did you use last time? How might it be useful this time?
- Which four numbers do you think could go in the grid to make it easy/hard to find reasons for each of the numbers to be unique? Explain why you are choosing those numbers.

Review and reflect

Check that your reason statements use mathematics vocabulary accurately.

How many of the reasons on the flipchart have you used? See if you can use another reason from the flipchart. If not, convince me why you cannot do that.

(Continued)

(Continued)

How many properties 'in common' have you found for pairs of numbers? See if you can use another number property from the flipchart. If not, convince me why you cannot do that.

Assessment

Ask a friend to check (or check yourself):

- that each of your reasons definitely makes that number unique
- that the properties 'in common' you have for two numbers are accurate.

How accurately have you used the mathematical vocabulary?

What new reasons and properties have you found?

What have you learnt about numbers from this activity?

Adapting the tasks for younger learners

Younger learners will benefit from focusing on what two of the numbers in the grid have in common and finding a unique number out of the four is the 'digging deeper' element for them. You may like to use a 1-3 dice and a 0-9 dice so that the numbers generated are all below 40 or you could choose numbers to go in the grid rather than generating them with dice.

The youngest learners can access the activity by using equipment, such as Numicon or Multilink, in the grid cells rather than numbers or using the numbers 1 to 20.

The youngest learners may talk about the shapes of the numerals such as: '3 and 8 both have curves'.

ACTIVITY

Awesome adding

No resources are needed for this example activity which can be used to introduce problem solving and reasoning into a standard lesson on calculation.

National curriculum and mathematical understanding links

Suitable for: Years 2 and 3; can be adapted for other year groups.

Objectives: to add two two-digit numbers, mentally where possible.

Mathematical understanding: addition of number, commutativity of addition and reasoning.

Setting the scene

44	85	71	20
27	14	39	41
58	15	23	46
35	70	28	52

Figure 4.3   'Awesome adding' grid

Draw the four-by-four grid in Figure 4.3 on the board so that all the children can see.

Explain that they are going to choose any two numbers from the grid to add together. There are six steps to this part of the activity as outlined below.

1. *Spot the easy calculations*

    Which two numbers would they choose so that the calculation is an easy one? Write their suggestions on the board, such as, 70 + 20, 41 + 20. Ask them to explain why they think it is easy.

    Encourage the children to give you answers that are complete sentences and use mathematical vocabulary correctly. For example, '70 add 20 is easy because they are multiples of ten.

    Invite the children to work out the answers and explain to you how they will check they are correct.

2. *Commutative*

    Ask the children if it matters which way round you write the numbers in the addition calculation? (41 + 20 is the same as 20 + 41 because addition is commutative. Encourage the children to use this mathematical word).

3. *Vocabulary*

    Ask the children to tell you different ways they could read the number sentence 41 + 20 = 61, such as, 'the total of 41 and 20 is 61'.

4. *Other similar calculations in the 'same family'*

    Choose one of their suggestions such as, '52 + 41 is easy to add as the tens add to less than one hundred and the ones add to less than ten' and ask them if they can find three other calculations that work in this way. For example, 44 + 14 and 52 + 23. Invite the children to work out the answers and explain to you how they will check they are correct.

5. *All in the grid*

    Challenge the children to see if they can find any addition calculations where the numbers that you add together and the answer are all in the grid (for example, 70 + 15 = 85).

6. *Spot the hard calculations*

    Ask the children to find two numbers that are harder to add together. Ask them to explain what makes the calculation harder. For example, '85 + 46 is harder because the sum of the

(Continued)

(Continued)

ones is greater than ten and the sum of the tens is greater than one hundred'. Ask them to find other calculations in the grid that are like this. Invite the children to work out the answers and explain to you how they will check if they are accurate.

Support

Encourage the use of apparatus and number lines to calculate the answers if needed.

Encourage children who find the harder ones a challenge to look for further easy ones in the grid.

Ask them if they can change one digit in a harder one to make it easier.

Invite them to explain how that would help. For example, '58 + 46 would be easier if it was 58 + 41 because the ones would add up to less than ten'.

Digging deeper (High Ceiling)

Some children will be ready for further challenges using the grid. This will depend on how they get on with the first activity. Invite them to work in pairs to make up their own four-by-four grid using these critieria:

- The grid has a mix of easy and hard calculations.
- The grid contains two sets of three numbers such that two of the three numbers can be added together to make the third.

To get a good grid is harder than you think! Invite pairs to swop grids and see if they can find four easy and four hard calculations plus the two complete number sentences that are contained in the grid.

You can also help the children to dig deeper by giving them some working backwards questions, such as, 'the answer is 100 – what are my two numbers?'

81	10	29	98
15	75	25	31
50	52	48	34
36	18	77	40

44	85	21	30
20	14	22	41
51	15	23	16
35	45	28	50

Figure 4.4   More 'Awesome adding' grid examples

Encourage the children to explain how they test out possible pairs of numbers. What helps them to decide which numbers could work? For example, they might say, the answer has no ones, so the ones in the starting numbers must add up to ten.

You may like to give an additional clue such as 'my two numbers are in the same row of the grid, or 'my two numbers are adjacent to each other'. Invite them to try this activity in pairs after you have modelled it. This challenge is helping the children to develop the problem-solving skill of working backwards as well as reasoning.

Trigger questions

- What do you notice about those two numbers?

- Tell me how you are adding those two numbers.

- If I choose this number, what number would you choose to make it an easy/hard calculation?

- Tell me why you think that addition is easy/hard?

- What do those two calculations have in common?

- What do you notice about all the easy/hard calculations?

Review and reflect

- Have you found both easy and hard addition calculations?

- How do you know that your number sentences are accurate?

- What makes a calculation easy or hard?

- Have you devised your own four-by-four grid successfully, using the criteria given?

- What tips would you give to someone else designing their own four-by-four grid?

Assessment questions

- What calculations have you chosen?

- Explain to me what makes them easy/hard for you.

- How do you know that you have calculated the answers accurately?

- Show me how the grid that you have designed fits the criteria given.

Adapting the task

To simplify the task, you may like to use smaller numbers or more multiples of ten and five. To increase the calculation demands, you can use larger numbers, decimal numbers, a mix of decimal numbers and fractions.

ACTIVITY

Addition trios

No resources are needed for this example activity which helps children develop their problem-solving skills and uses mathematical content that is likely to be within their comfort zone.

National curriculum and mathematical understanding links

Suitable for: Years 3 and 4 or Years 5 and 6 if they have limited experience of working systematically.

Objectives: to learn to work systematically (part of the problem-solving aim).

Mathematical understanding: the problem-solving skill of working systematically, addition number sentences and the commutativity of addition. Since the demands of working systematically are high and it is the focus of the lesson, it is good to use mathematical content that is well within the grasp of the children.

Setting the scene

Draw the four-by-four grid in Figure 4.5 on the board so that all the children can see.

3	8	6	16
23	4	12	5
9	2	7	15
14	20	27	11

Figure 4.5   Addition trios grid

Explain that they are going to work in pairs to find as many addition trios as they can from the grid.

Explain that an addition trio is a set of three numbers where two of them can be added together to make the third. For example, 3 + 6 = 9.

Exploring the grid

Give the pairs of children around ten minutes to explore the grid and find as many addition trios as they can. Draw the class back together to discuss the issue of whether 3 + 6 = 9 is the same addition trio as 6 + 3 = 9. Ensure that you use the word commutative when explaining to the children that these are the same trio because addition can be done in any order. Ask the children whether they need to cross out any trios on their list as they are the same.

See if anyone in the class has thought about whether you can use the same number twice. If not, suggest a trio of 2 + 2 = 4 and ask the children if they think that is a suitable addition trio. It is up to the class to decide whether it is or not. You may prefer to stick to the rule of using numbers only once to limit the number of possible addition trios.

Draw from the class different types of recording they have used for their trios. Discuss the benefits and disadvantages of each. Let the children decide if they want to carry on using the recording strategy that they started with or 'magpie' another one that you have discussed. For example, (3, 6, 9) is one way of recording the three numbers in the addition trio.

Let the pairs of children continue to explore the grid with the challenge this time of finding how many addition trios there are. The challenge is, 'How do you know that you have found them all?'

Draw the class back together and invite a child who thinks their pair has found them all to read out their list. Others can cross the addition trios off their list if they have them. This is likely to result in a degree of confusion as others hunt for a trio in their list. Stop the child who is reading out their list and explain that we need a way of working systematically (having a pattern) so that it is easier to see if we have them all. Invite the pairs of children to look at their lists and see if they can reorder them using a pattern. There will be more than one way of doing this.

While the pairs of children are working on this further, circulate around the class and choose a pair that has a clear pattern to come to the front and share their pattern. A visualizer is a great way of sharing children's work. The pair do not need to have found all the trios. They may still be using their pattern to work on that. Discuss with the class what their pattern is and how this could help find all the addition trios. Ask the class who has a different pattern to share and invite them to come to the front to show the class. Discuss with the class the advantages of having a pattern and how it will help us know that we have found all the possible number trios. This is a key problem-solving skill and children benefit from becoming familiar with it as early as possible.

Let the pairs of children work further on using a pattern to find all the possible addition trios. They can 'magpie' another pairs' pattern if that is useful to them. Some children will get as far as learning to use a pattern and others (possibly a few) will be able to find all the addition trios.

Invite a pair to the front to share their solution. Ask the children if they agree or disagree with the number of addition trios found. Discuss with the class how their pattern convinces us (or not) that they have found them all. This may require some dedicated time to help all children understand and articulate the reasoning process. This is an important part of the lesson.

Here is one way of working systematically: start with the smallest number and increase the next number by one each time, as long as that number and the answer number are in the grid. This assumes that each number can only be used once in any addition trio.

(2, 3, 5) (2, 4, 6) (2, 5, 7) (2, 6, 8) (2, 7, 9) (2, 9, 11) (2, 12, 14) (2, 14, 16)

We then start with 3 and work upwards as (3, 2, 5) has already been counted.

This is because addition is commutative.

(3, 4, 7) (3, 5, 8) (3, 6, 9) (3, 8, 11) (3, 9, 12) (3, 11, 14) (3, 12, 15) (3, 20, 23)

(4, 5, 9) (4, 7, 11) (4, 8, 12) (4, 11, 15) (4, 12, 16) (4, 16, 20) (4, 23, 27)

(5, 6, 11) (5, 7, 12) (5, 9, 14) (5, 11, 16) (5, 15, 20)

(6, 8, 14) (6, 9, 15) (6, 14, 20)

(Continued)

(Continued)

(7, 8, 15) (7, 9, 16) (7, 16, 23) (7, 20, 27)

(8, 12, 20) (8, 15, 23)

(9, 11, 20) (9, 14, 23)

(11, 12, 23) (11, 16, 27)

(12, 15, 27)

Total: 42 addition trios

Digging deeper (High Ceiling)

Invite pairs of children to design a four-by-four addition trio grid containing more addition trios than the one they have been working with so far. Which numbers are helpful numbers that are found in a lot of trios? Which numbers are only found in a few trios?

See if the children start with a new grid of numbers or if they adjust the one they have been working with so far. The latter is a 'smart' way of tackling the challenge and uses the problem-solving skill of trial and improvement. For example, if we remove 27, we lose four addition number trios. They can then explore different replacements for 27.

For example, 13 offers four addition trios: (2, 11, 13) (4, 9, 13) (5, 8, 13) (6, 7, 13) so this is no help; 18 offers five addition trios: (2, 16, 18) (3, 15, 18) (4, 14, 18) (6, 12, 18) (7, 11, 18). Thus replacing 27 with 18 will increase the number of addition trios by one.

3	8	6
11	4	12
9	2	7
3	8	6
11	4	12
9	2	7

Figure 4.6   Addition trios grid designed by children

Support

Offer the children a smaller grid for the same activity. Here is one way of working systematically to find a solution:

2	11	8
7	4	3
12	9	6

Figure 4.7   A Smaller addition trios grid

(2, 4, 6) (2, 6, 8) (2, 9, 11)

(3, 4, 7) (3, 6, 9) (3, 8, 11) (3, 9, 12)

(4, 7, 11) (4, 8, 12)

Ask the children to explain why there is no possibility of trios beginning with 6.

Note: you may like to use a similar three-by-three grid to model ways of working systematically with the class if this is a new, or relatively new, skill for them.

Trigger questions

- Convince me that these are addition number trios.

- How do you know that each of your addition number trios is different?

- What pattern are you using to help you find them all?

- How is your pattern helping you to find the addition number trios?

- What convinces you that you have found them all?

- What can you do to increase the number of addition number trios that you can find from the grid?

Review and reflect

Convince yourself that all your addition number trios are unique and that you have no repeats.

What pattern are you using to help you find them all?

How far have you got with finding them all?

What will enable you to find a grid with more addition number trios than this one?

Assessment

How do you know that you have found some accurate addition number trios?

How do you know that you have no repeats?

What convinces you that you have found all the possible addition number trios?

What did you do to find a grid with more addition number trios than this one?

Adapting the tasks

You may like to use smaller three-by-three or three-by-four grids to reduce the number of addition number trios.

To take the tasks further you may like to move on to multiplication trios, using the same structure as above.

FOLLOW-UP ACTIVITIES AND TASKS

The following are freely available from NRICH, University of Cambridge: www.nrich.maths.org:

Strike it out https://nrich.maths.org/6589. Use strategic thinking plus addition and subtraction skills to play this game. Can you cross out all the numbers?

Maze 100 http://nrich.maths.org/91. Can you go through this maze so that the numbers you pass add up exactly to 100?

Reach 100 http://nrich.maths.org/1130. Choose four different digits from 1–9 and place them in the boxes so that the total of the four two-digit numbers is exactly 100.

REFERENCES

Alexander, **RJ** and **Armstrong**, **M** (2010) *Children, Their World, Their Education: Final Report of the Cambridge Primary Review*. London: Routledge.

Papert, **S** (1980) *Mindstorms: Children, Computers, and Powerful Ideas*. New York: Basic Books.

FURTHER READING

McClure, Lynne (2012) 'Using Low Threshold High Ceiling activities in primary classrooms', NRICH, University of Cambridge. Available at: https://nrich.maths.org/8768.

Alexander, Robin (2012), 'Improving oracy and classroom talk in English schools: achievements and challenges', University of Cambridge. Available at: www.robinalexander.org.uk/wp-content/uploads/2012/06/DfE-oracy-120220-Alexander-FINAL.pdf (accessed May 2016).

5

STORIES AND MATHEMATICS

CHERRI MOSELEY

IN THIS CHAPTER

This chapter:

- explores how mathematics can be taught through quality stories and children's literature
- considers how story can be used to help children develop understanding of concepts
- highlights how stories can provide a safe space for children to make mistakes and learn from them
- includes classroom activities that use visual representations of number and shape to complement storytelling.

For thousands of years, stories have been used to teach. In days gone by, a story might have perpetuated people's traditions, told of a great event or passed on essential survival information. Beginning as an oral tradition, storytelling soon progressed to include actions, images and much more.

Nowadays, we continue to appreciate stories through books, television, radio, films and games. Many stories are beautifully captured within children's books and are easily available. In school, we use stories in many different formats to teach, exploiting the fact that children love stories across the whole curriculum including mathematics. An appropriate story can be used to support the introduction and development of a concept, to set a problem to be solved and to summarize or consolidate learning. A story can set the scene for you and your class to exploit.

Stories are engaging and highly motivating. Children enjoy hearing, reading and discussing a story. It makes the concepts more accessible and quickly keys the children in when revisiting. Mistakes are non-threatening and stories encourage risk taking as children suggest what a character could do. Stories are often cross-curricular and range from the profound to the practical. Animating a story by acting it out with props and carrying out linked activities helps to embed the underlying ideas and concepts, that is, to teach.

This chapter offers a few examples of stories to engage children in mathematics, but it would be impossible to list all the useful books. Arguably, you could use any story, just read it with your own mathematical eyes open and you will be surprised what you find.

ACTIVITY

Number

Mouse Count (by Ellen Stoll Walsh)

Suitable for: Early Years

Synopsis: A hungry snake searches for a meal. A single mouse is simply not enough, so the snake collects sleepy mice in a discarded jar to make a decent meal. Deciding that three, and then seven are not enough, the snake continues to collect mice until there are ten in the jar. The snake is about to eat when one of the mice wakes up and points out a large mouse some distance away. As the snake rushes off to add to his meal, the mice throw themselves at one side of the jar, then the opposite side repeatedly. The jar rocks and falls, allowing the mice to 'uncount' themselves from the jar. The large mouse turns out to be a rock and the snake is left hungry.

Setting the scene

With a jar, ten mouse-shaped catnip cat toys or finger puppets and a snake puppet, act out the story as you read it. Pause frequently to count how many mice are in the jar, giving the children repeated opportunities to recount the mice. When the snake disappears to go after the large mouse, rock the jar backwards and forwards until it tips over. Remind the children that there were ten in the jar and 'uncount' the mice as they escape from the jar.

You have set the scene for numerous counting to ten and counting back from ten activities. This could include focused group activities with children taking the parts of the mice and snake or using puppets. Leaving the props available for children to use ensures that they will continue to act out the story, practising counting (and 'uncounting') repeatedly. They may well adapt and change the story, but that does not matter; they will still be practising their counting.

Ten is such a key number in our number system that it is useful for children to know as much about it as they can. Having counted to ten and back to zero, you can also explore ten in many different ways. Having alerted the children to count to and from ten, introduce them to the ten frame. There are two different versions. The first is the standard five-by-two grid.

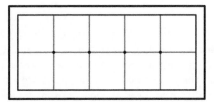

Figure 5.1   Ten frame

The Hungarian ten frame is arranged in two fives, which is very useful for exploring five or more. This frame helps children to recognize the layout of five on dice or dominoes.

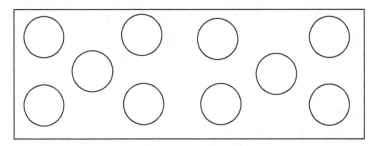

Figure 5.2   Hungarian ten frame

Tasks

Use the ten frame as a mat for children to work on. Both are easily made, though they can also be bought. If you make them yourself, you can print them out on yellow paper as cheese for the mice to nibble at. When you move on from mice, the ten frame could be blue, perhaps a pond for frogs or green, a field for horses. Repeating the counting with a variety of objects helps children to understand that numbers behave in the same way, whatever is being counted. This solid grounding helps to build an image of ten and numbers to ten that will support children's understanding of our number system.

Initially, the children can count the mice onto the ten frame, placing one in each square, or on each circle. This will enable you to check children have secure one-to-one correspondence. The next step is to pause part way through the count and ask children, 'How many more do we need to make ten?' Children can quickly see and count how many empty places there are. Some children may be able to subitize, that is, know how many without counting. This is a very useful skill for children to develop, though it will be limited to small numbers at first. Model the number statement as, for example, seven mice and three more mice make ten mice altogether. You could also use different colours, so it could be seven brown mice and three red mice make ten mice altogether. When the children are ready, model writing the number statement and encourage some children to write it for themselves on a whiteboard.

Follow-up tasks

Move on to explore subtraction as take away. With all ten mice on the ten frame, remove one and verbalize the number statement 'ten mice take away one mouse leaves nine mice'. Just as with

(Continued)

(Continued)

addition, model the number statement and encourage children to write it for themselves. You may want to link addition and subtraction, showing $9 + 1 = 10$ and $10 - 1 = 9$, doing the addition and undoing by subtracting. You could use the language doing and undoing or even introduce the more mathematical 'inverse'. The opportunities for recording are endless. On a paper ten frame, children can use bingo dabbers, crosses, ticks, stampers or something else. These can be stuck into a child's book or children can record on a ten frame stamped into their book. Some children could write the number statement alongside – much depends on the children you are working with.

As children extend their understanding to 20, use ten frames in pairs. Begin by counting objects onto the frames, one in each space. Always fill one ten frame before moving on to the second one. Pause to confirm that 11 is ten and one more, and so on all the way to 20. Number bonds for 20 can be explored in exactly the same way as they were for ten. For other numbers, cut some squares off the ten frame. By consistently using the pattern of twos as a whole row or column (depending on the orientation of the tens frame), odd numbers always have an unmatched space, while even numbers are rectangles. So if the children are to explore 12, use a ten frame and a two frame. This helps to reinforce that 12 is ten and two.

Review and reflect

Eventually, the ten frame becomes an image of ten in its own right and children no longer need to place an object in each space. Use it to support counting in tens. There is so much you can do with some simple paper ten frames.

Once you have found an author that you like, it is worth exploring what else they have to offer. *Mouse Shapes* and *Mouse Paint* by Ellen Stoll Walsh are just as useful, both within mathematics and across the curriculum.

ACTIVITY

One Is a Snail Ten Is a Crab (by April Pulley Sayre and Jeff Sayre)

Suitable for: Key Stages 1 and 2

Synopsis: Since one is a snail and two is a person, we must be counting by feet. Using a dog for four, an insect for six, a spider for eight and a crab for ten, the book counts from one to one hundred and gives some amusing pictures to enjoy along the way.

Setting the scene

Read and enjoy the story with the children, encouraging them to predict how the next number will be shown. They will enjoy being caught out as the counting switches from ones to tens – there are no teen numbers in the book. This book is a gift for exploring teen numbers, multiples of ten and partitioning numbers in different ways.

Tasks

Inevitably, when you reach the last page, a child will ask, 'Are there really 100 snails?' Straight away, you have a group activity. With the book flat on the table, ask the children how you could check. It will not be difficult to get in a muddle! If the children do not suggest it, you can encourage them to place a cube on each snail. Then, collect the cubes and put them into ten sticks, or place them on ten frames. Then count in tens to check that there are indeed 100 snails.

Make several laminated pictures of each creature, about the size of your hand to make them clearly visible or clone images on the whiteboard. Using crabs and snails as tens and ones, partition teen numbers into tens and ones to create the missing pages. It is useful to prepare simple paper stamps of crabs and snails using clipart for children to use so that they do not spend a long time drawing when recording, although they should always have that option. Clipart stamps are particularly useful when moving on to use the other creatures. A child's drawing of an insect can be indistinguishable from their drawing of a spider, though hopefully each has the correct number of legs! Challenge children to make the same number in two or three different ways. You can differentiate your choice of number according to the level of challenge each child will respond to, giving each child a number card or cloakroom ticket with their number on to explore.

Use your laminated creatures to create addition and subtraction statements for children to solve, including missing creature statements. Challenge them to create their own, either drawing or using clip art stamps, with, for example, a total of 23 or a difference of 11.

Children can also explore which numbers can be made with only one creature. Begin with numbers to ten first of all. Ask the children to help you list the numbers that can be made with only one creature and those that need two. Ask what is different about your two lists. Use the discussion to introduce or consolidate odd and even numbers. You could go on to discuss why creatures always have an even number of feet, except a snail, and ask if the same is true for wings. Extend the exploration to larger numbers. This could lead on to creating the multiplication tables for 1, 2, 4, 6, 8 and 10 as appropriate. Creating multiplication tables in this way has the advantage of starting from the creature. So if a child is using crabs, then four of them naturally leads to the matching repeated addition and/or multiplication statement.

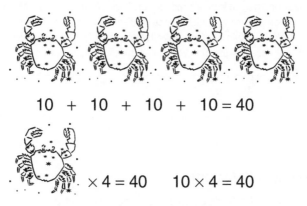

$$10 + 10 + 10 + 10 = 40$$

$$\times 4 = 40 \qquad 10 \times 4 = 40$$

Figure 5.3 Using crabs to count in tens

(Continued)

(Continued)

Follow-up tasks

Child-made multiplication tables in this format make a useful display. Make links between 10 × 4 = 40 (four crabs) and 4 × 10 = 40 (ten dogs). The product is the same, but the two collections of creatures are very different. It also helps children to recognize that multiplication is more efficient, including much less writing than repeated addition.

$$4 + 4 + 4 + 4 + 4 + 4 + 4 + 4 + 4 + 4 = 40$$

× 10 = 40   4 × 10 = 40

Figure 5.4   Using dogs to count in fours

Use your laminated pictures to create a different number at the beginning or end of each session. Challenge children to quickly tell you the total number of feet and then tell the class a different way to make the same number of feet. Ask for another and another and another before introducing a different number or asking a child to suggest one. You can also ask if a particular number can be made, for example, with only crabs or only dogs. Ask children to explain how they know.

Review and reflect

The beauty of this book is that it shows children that there are numbers within numbers, helping children to develop a more fluent understanding of number. You do not have to stick with feet. Enjoy the book and if you are in the middle of a transport topic, then use wheels instead. One is a unicycle or wheelbarrow, two is a bicycle, three is a tricycle or rickshaw, four is a car. Five is a car with a spare wheel on the back or a unicycle on the roof. For six, eight and ten, explore the arrangement of wheels on different vehicles including fire engines, refuse trucks, cement mixers and so on. Vehicles with a heavy load often have two pairs of four wheels with two further wheels on the cab, a total of ten wheels. I am sure you can think of many other possibilities.

ACTIVITY

The Rabbit Problem (by Emily Gravett)

Synopsis: The book takes the form of a calendar, beginning in January with a single lonely rabbit. After a mate arrives in February, twins Alfafa and Angora are born in March. As another pair arrives, the population begins to grow. Thankfully, the field is labelled with how many pairs of rabbits it contains as it becomes more and more difficult to count them all.

Setting the scene

This is the perfect book to convince older children that they have not outgrown picture books. It has lots of added extras, including a newspaper, a knitting pattern, a recipe book, a ration book and more. A ruler is used to measure the depth of water in the field and a tape measure for a bunny check-up. A thermometer is used to measure how hot it is.

Tasks

Children could track the number of rabbits in Fibonacci's field at the beginning of each month (1, 1, 2, 3, 5, 8, 13, 21...). Ask children how the numbers are linked and challenge them to continue the sequence. They could also make a poster of the growth in rabbit population in Fibonacci's field:

January population 1 rabbit, February population 1 pair of rabbits, March population 2 pairs of rabbits, April population 3 pairs of rabbits ...

The Fibonacci sequence is an example of efficiency in nature. As each row of seeds in a sunflower or pine cone, or petals on a flower grows, the plant tries to put the maximum number in the smallest space. Fibonacci numbers are the whole numbers that express the golden ratio that corresponds to the angle that maximizes the number of items in the smallest space. The seed head and petals of a sunflower, daisies and pine cones have two sets of spirals, one radiating clockwise and the other anti-clockwise.

Produce some pictures for children to examine. Ask, How many clockwise spirals in each plant? How many anti-clockwise spirals in each plant? Are they always Fibonacci numbers? A quick internet search will direct you to websites with more information on the topic (for example, see Ron Knott in 'Further reading' at the end of this chapter).

Follow-up tasks

Make the Fibonacci squares and spirals patterns. Squares equal in size to the Fibonacci numbers fit together to make a growing pattern. Children will need to decide how big the '1 square' is – 1cm or 2cm squared paper is ideal for this.

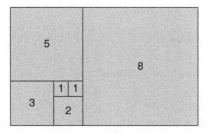

Figure 5.5   Fibonacci squares

Once children have created Fibonacci squares, they can draw in the spiral.

(Continued)

(Continued)

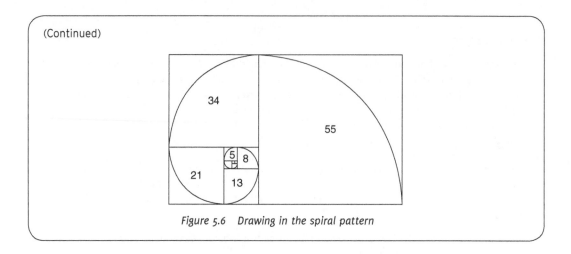

Figure 5.6   Drawing in the spiral pattern

FURTHER BOOKS FOR NUMBER

The books above are just a few examples of useful stories for exploring number and what you might do with them. There are many more. *Use One Grain of Rice: A Mathematical Folktale* by Demi to explore doubling and halving. Children are always amazed by how quickly numbers grow when doubling. Make doubling streets or blocks of flats, where each house number is double the one before. Start with 100 or 1000 and repeatedly halve it, extending into fractions and later, decimals. Challenge children to find a starting number that they can repeatedly halve to reach $\frac{1}{2}$.

One Hundred Hungry Ants by Elinor J. Pinczes is useful for exploring multiplication and division. Can 100 be divided exactly by 2, 5, 10, 20, 25 and 50? Cut up blank 100 squares ten-by-ten grids without numbers) to find out, and support children to complete matching multiplication and division statements. As with number statements using creatures in *One Is a Snail Ten Is a Crab*, children will soon see the link between statements such as $100 \div 2 = 50$, $100 \div 50 = 2$, $2 \times 50 = 100$, $50 \times 2 = 100$. Explore how these can also be written as $100 = 2 \times 50$, $100 = 50 \times 2$, $2 = 100 \div 50$ and $50 = 100 \div 2$. If you are ready to explore remainders, then move on to explore dividing 100 by each number up to 12 and perhaps beyond. Follow up with *A Remainder of One* also by Pinczes.

365 Penguins by Jean-Luc Fromental is one of those books that can be used for a whole range of mathematics, science and writing. Questions such as 'Why do penguins stand in the shade?' will arise from exploring the pictures. As you share the last page with the children, their imagination will already have begun to run riot with the next story. Before you get to that point, children could write persuasive emails to the anonymous sender who has accidentally left an email address on the back of one of the labels, perhaps penguins@southpole.com. The emails should become increasingly desperate as the total number of penguins increases, asking children to think carefully about the language they use. As for the mathematics, challenge children to draw up a table showing the total number of penguins at the end of each month. What will be the date when 100 penguins have arrived? Ask how they would organize the penguins on a particular day. Dad's solution on 4 August was a cube, $6 \times 6 \times 6$. How many penguins were there on 4 August? When could Dad make different-sized cubes? Start with one penguin, which is $1 \times 1 \times 1 = 1^3$, on 1 January.

How much fish is needed and how much will it cost to feed the penguins on a particular day? 365 is the smallest number that can be written as a sum of consecutive squares in more than 1 way. 1, 4, 9, 16, 25, 36, 49, ... are square numbers. Challenge children to work together to find at least two sums of consecutive squares that total 365. Many other questions will occur to you and the children as you share the story. This book is particularly useful for a school wide topic because it can be explored in so many different ways.

Another whole school book is *At Our House* by Isabel Minhos Martins and Madalena Matoso. This time the focus is on parts of the body from bones to tongues and how many of each are in your home, including pets. Every child could make their own *At Our House* booklet, exploring addition and multiples according to the number of people and creatures in their home.

And finally, *Daisy and the Trouble with Zoos* by Kes Grey has a very Interesting take on fractions in Chapter 1 and *Nigel's Numberless World* by Lucy Coats really makes you think about what we use numbers for in everyday life.

MEASURES

ACTIVITY

Would You Rather ... (by John Burningham)

Synopsis: Each single- or double-page spread offers the reader some choices. For example, would you rather be made to eat ... spider stew, slug dumplings, mashed worms or drink snail squash? Alternatively, would you rather have ... a monkey to tickle, a bear to read to, a cat to box with, a dog to skate with, a pig to ride or a goat to dance with? It ends by asking if you would rather just go to sleep in your own bed - a fitting ending after considering all the options in the book.

Setting the scene

The book will generate many Yuk! and Never! comments but can also be the starting point for many discussions. Most of these are more about personal preference than mathematics but having read the book, you can use the same format to set some mathematical challenges, particularly those involving measures.

Tasks

You could start by writing recipes for spider stew, slug dumplings, mashed worms or snail squash, using the appropriate measure for each ingredient and finding the total mass of stew, dumplings or mash. For snail squash, both grams (or kilograms) and millilitres (or litres) will be needed and again, the totals can be found. Towards the end, the book asks 'Would you rather live with ... a gerbil in a cage, a fish in a bowl, a parrot on a perch, a rabbit in a hutch, chickens in a coop or a dog in a kennel?' Challenge children to draw a scaled diagram of their chosen living space. They will need

(Continued)

(Continued)

to consider how big the space needs to be for them to stand up and lie down in. They may need to measure their height and will certainly need to consider what scale to use for their drawing and what size paper they will need. Other considerations such as, 'Would square or plain paper be more useful?' could be discussed as a class.

Having followed up on some of the 'Would you rather…' questions in the book, you can easily move on to designing your own questions to explore the relevant areas of the curriculum. For a combination of money and length, you could ask, 'Would you rather have a metre of 5p coins or 30cm of 10p coins?' and 'How can you find out which is worth the most?' Alternatively, children could write their name using coins, then consider the challenge, 'Would you rather have your first name "written" in 20p coins or your full name "written" in 2p coins?' and 'How can you find out which is worth the most?'

Other comparisons could focus on mass or capacity. For example, 'Would you rather have $\frac{1}{10}$ of a 1 kg cake or $\frac{1}{4}$ of a 500g cake?' or 'Would you rather have 300ml or $\frac{1}{4}$ of a litre of your favourite drink?' Such comparisons are easily extended across the mathematics curriculum, including fractions and percentages. For example, if the squares on all bars of chocolate are the same size, 'Would you rather have $\frac{1}{3}$ of a ten squares-by-three squares bar or $\frac{1}{2}$ of a four squares-by-five squares bar?' Alternatively, 'Would you rather have 5% of £10 or 75% of 80p?' or 'Would you rather be given 25% of five pizzas or 40% of three pizzas?' For time, it could be, 'Would you rather wait for $\frac{1}{3}$ of two hours or 50% of an hour?' The possibilities are endless.

FURTHER BOOKS FOR MEASURES

Other useful stories for measures include *Jim and the Beanstalk* by Raymond Briggs. Use this to compare measurements for children and giants. *Millions to Measure* by David M Schwartz is useful for exploring Imperial and metric measures. For time, there's *Tom and the Tinful of Trouble* by Nick Sharratt and *Just a Second* by Steve Jenkins for comparing units of time. *Bear Takes a Trip* by Sheila Blackstone is useful for hours and quarter hours, am and pm as well as both analogue and digital time, while *Clocks and More Clocks* by Pat Hutchins is useful for exploring minutes. For percentages, try *If the World Were a Village* by David J Smith.

SHAPE

ACTIVITY

The Greedy Triangle (by Marilyn Burns)

Synopsis: Although the triangle is always on the go and keen to catch up with the local gossip, it gets dissatisfied with doing the same things day after day. A visit to the local shapeshifter adds one more side and one more angle and it is happy again. But not for long. The repeated visits to the shapeshifter gradually transform the triangle into other shapes until it suffers from a major identity crisis.

Setting the scene

This book is all about polygons and defines them for you in the information at the back of the book. A polygon is a 2D shape with straight sides and is named according to its number of angles (or 'knees' – knees is the direct translation of 'gon'). A triangle's witty growth into a decagon allows some serious consideration of the properties of 2D shapes.

There is much to be gained from not rushing this story. As you share the first two double page spreads, encourage children to notice the various triangles in the pictures and to spot triangles around the room. Explain that the word triangle means three angles, and a shape with three angles must have three sides. Move on to the two quadrilateral spreads, listing the different kinds of quadrilaterals the book mentions. Since the book is about a greedy triangle, it makes sense to start the activities by making triangles. Using geo strips or strips of card the same length (15cm long and 1cm wide is perfect) and split pins, ask children to make a triangle. Then give everyone another strip of the same length to add to their shape. Talk about what they have made (a rhombus), including when it is a square (equal angles) and when it is not, that is, when the angles are not all equal. Reinforce the fact that 2D shapes with four sides are called quadrilaterals (four sides as opposed to four angles).

As you read further pages in the book, give children another strip to add to their shape, replicating the actions of the shapeshifter. Talk about the new shape made and explore both regular and irregular shapes. To avoid confusion, explore shapes using strips all the same length at first. Then introduce strips of different lengths and explore how the shapes are the same and how they are different. When doing this with quadrilaterals, you could ask children to make as many different quadrilaterals as they can. Finish the activity by asking each pair to contribute a different quadrilateral to the quadrilateral family. Name them where you can and use them to make a great shape display.

Follow this up by going on a square hunt around the school. You could even change the popular 'We're going on a Bear Hunt' to 'We're going on a Square Hunt' to add to the fun! Take examples of squares with you to check the angles if it is too early to introduce right angles, and tape measures to measure the sides to check they are all the same length. Photograph the square in its location and create a book or file of squares. Do the same for other shapes once you have read the rest of the book but beware – there will be many examples of some shapes and none of others. The PE cupboard is usually a good source of both 2D and 3D shapes. If all else fails, pin some shapes up around the school for the children to find.

As you read the rest of the book, draw up a list of the name of each shape, linking it to the number of sides and angles. Children could work in a group to make a shape sequence, starting with a triangle and adding one more side to create the next shape. Shapes could be stuck to a long, wide strip of paper and labelled. Children could also explore a single shape such as a hexagon and make a hexagon family by changing the orientation of the sides. Swap one or more sides for different lengths to make an even bigger family.

(Continued)

(Continued)

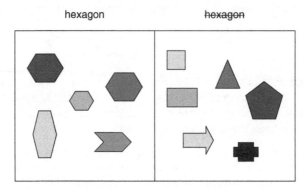

hexagon   ~~hexagon~~

Figure 5.7   Using a Carroll diagram to sort polygons

Sort polygons according to their properties. Use a Carroll diagram to sort regular polygons by name, for example, hexagon and ~~hexagon~~ to help reinforce the appropriate shape. The same caption is used for the second box but crossed out to mean 'not'. You could either stick to regular polygons or extend to irregular polygons for a particular number of sides.

If you have shapes in a range of colours, as in a set of logic blocks for example, use a Carroll diagram to sort for two attributes, colour and shape. It is the doing that matters, so record by taking photographs. Make into a sorting book.

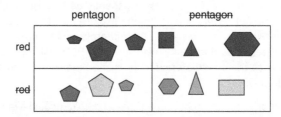

pentagon   ~~pentagon~~

red

~~red~~

Figure 5.8   Using a Carroll diagram to sort coloured polygons

Give groups of children a named picture of a polygon. Challenge the groups to create a scene with as many copies of their polygon as they can manage. This makes a fun display. You could go on to look at symmetry and fractions of shapes; explore tessellation and look at Escher pictures; make pictures with tangrams or regular polygons related to any current topic and much more than there is room to suggest here.

FURTHER BOOKS FOR SHAPE

Many books use shapes to create pictures or to explore shapes in the environment, including *The Shape of Things* by Dayle Ann Dodds, *A Triangle for Adaora* by Ifeoma Onyefulu and *Bear in a Square* by Sheila Blackstone. *The Silly Story of Goldie Locks and the Three Squares* by Grace Maccarone really is silly, but good fun too. When it comes to the properties of a circle, *Sir Cumference and the Dragon of Pi* and *Sir Cumference and the Knights of the First Round Table*, both by Cindy Neuschwander, explore the properties of a circle in a fun way that clearly explains the vocabulary used. There are fewer books for 3D shapes, but *Captain Invincible and the Space Shapes* by Stuart J. Murphy is useful.

Fashions change in mathematics just as much as they do elsewhere. It is becoming more fashionable to use the correct mathematical terms for everything, regardless of the age of the children. Many of these books were not written with that in mind, so you will need to introduce the correct mathematical vocabulary to supplement the terms used in the books. This is likely to include vertex and vertices for corner or corners, apex for the point of a cone and curved surfaces rather than curved faces.

Books go out of print all the time, but there is a lively second-hand market out there. If you search using an online retailer, they will often recommend other books. If you can see inside it online, you can often get a good idea as to whether or not it will be useful. You may buy the odd duff book, but it is worth the risk. It is also worth exploring what you already have, looking for the mathematics within the story. It is often there, even if you did not notice it the first time round. Do browse the school library. There is unlikely to be a section labelled Mathematics, and even if there is, there are unlikely to be many stories. So just take a random pile and have a flick through with your mathematical hat on. You will be surprised at what you will find. Good hunting!

FURTHER READING

Briggs, M and **Davis, S** (2008) *Creative Teaching Mathematics in the Early Years and Primary Classrooms.* Abingdon: Routledge.

Knott, R (2016) Website on Fibonacci numbers and nature, http://www.maths.surrey.ac.uk/hosted-sites/R.Knott/Fibonacci/fibnat.html

McGrath, C (2014) *Teaching Mathematics Through Story.* Abingdon: Routledge.

Pound, L and **Lee, T** (2011) *Teaching Mathematics Creatively.* Abingdon: Routledge.

Zazkis, R and **Liljedahl, P** (2009) *Teaching Mathematics as Storytelling.* Rotterdam: Sense Publishers.

6

EXPLOITING DIGITAL TECHNOLOGY IN MATHEMATICS

PABLO MAYORGA

IN THIS CHAPTER

This chapter

- helps you to understand the place of technology in learning
- shows you how to use digital technology to enhance children's deeper understanding
- supports your use of mobile technologies in the classroom
- introduces some free applications for you to use
- includes recommended websites for resources and further information.

The massive ambitions we share, as a nation, for education cannot be met without technology. Crucially, they cannot be met without technology designed to help people learn.

(Richard Noss, 2012, p2)

The report by the Technology Enhanced Learning Research Programme (Gillen and Barton, 2010) is clear about the place of technology within learning. There is a plethora of websites and an increasing number of educational apps that can have real impact on children's learning and achievement. Many schools are moving away from the once ubiquitous ICT suite to more mobile and recent digital technologies such as tablet computers (iOS-based or Android-based), laptops and netbooks such as Chrome books and even more recently, social media and collaborative platforms like Google Drive/Classroom or Wikispaces. It can be challenging to navigate this vast 'digital ocean' of resources and find the right one, whether it be a website, the latest app or the choice between a laptop or an iPad, which will allow teachers to 'exploit' the potential of available technology to the benefit of children's learning.

The activities in this chapter draw on clear and explicit digital technology use that enhances children's deep understanding of mathematical concepts. They draw on freely available resources, chosen because they allow children to experiment and model mathematical concepts explicitly in clear contrast with thousands of web-based games that simply check children's recall of facts (for example, multiplication facts, number bonds) and their speed in retrieving these facts.

Research has looked at the way teachers interact with technology and has developed theories and frameworks to describe these interactions from different perspectives (Clark-Wilson et al., 2014) but at the same time it has highlighted the challenges faced by the evolving role of teachers within an increasingly digitized classroom environment. The report *Primary Mathematics with ICT: A pupil's entitlement to ICT in primary mathematics* (BeCTA, 2009) in collaboration with the Mathematical Association and the Association of Teachers of Mathematics, identified some clear benefits for the mathematics classroom: learning from feedback; observing patterns and seeing connections; exploring data; 'teaching' the computer and developing visual imagery. However, with the advent of social media as well as the increasingly easy access to the World Wide Web via not just computers but smartphones and games consoles, issues of e-safety must be considered at all times and children have to be aware of the benefits and the potential dangers.

ACTIVITY

It's not fair!

Resources

- picnic pictures
- iPads with installed (free) app Shadow Puppet Edu by Seesaw Learning Inc:
- http://get-puppet.co./Available from iTunes store: **https://itunes.apple.com/gb/app/shadow-puppet-edu/id888504640?mt=8**
- Google Drive link to picnic pictures: **https://goo.gl/s1ohol**.

National curriculum and mathematical understanding links

Suitable for: age 5 and above.

Objectives: to reason about fair sharing and fractions as quotients.

(Continued)

(Continued)

Mathematical understanding: partitioning with fractions, equal/fair sharing, fractions as quotients and reasoning with fractions.

Fractions is a challenging topic in mathematics and research in the UK and USA (Behr et al., 1992; Nunes and Bryant, 2009; Lamon, 2007) has shown how hard it can be for learners to develop rational number sense which in turn leads to an understanding (or lack) of proportional reasoning and high-order mathematics in secondary school. Fair sharing builds on children's 'sense' of fairness and sharing and their informal pre-school knowledge.

Setting the scene

In the context of a Teddy Bears' picnic, introduce the activity explaining that Baby Bear is as hungry as Father Bear and Mother Bear and that it is not fair that he is going to get less of the picnic. For children to reason about fair sharing and partitioning with fractions, they need to explain aloud how they are sharing the picnic equally.

Before the lesson, some pictures of picnics need to be available for children (see 'Resources' above to access copyright-free pictures). The picnic pictures can be preloaded to the 'camera roll' on iPads, or they can be printed out in advance, or children can take the pictures themselves. As this activity is easily adapted, children can use plastic food to set up a picnic and then take a picture.

Briefly model the tools from Shadow Puppet Edu so children can use them to explain how they would help Baby Bear to have a fair share of the picnic. Choose the 'create new' option on the home page. This will take children to the 'add photos/videos' options.

Once children have chosen the picnic pictures, select 'next' and users will be taken to the first page of the presentation. Press 'record' at the bottom of the page and the 'drawing tools' menu appears on the right-hand side.

Drawing Tools menu

Figure 6.1   Drawing Tools menu from Shadow Puppet Edu

Children record how they will share equally the picnic while at the same time they use one of the drawing tools to show how they will share equally among the bears. Children should carry out this task in pairs or threes at the start. It can be adapted so children can then set their own picnic and show how they will share it equally. The link provided in this activity has pictures of several picnics as well as the individual items that make up these picnics. It is intended that children show how to share equally each of the items so that they partition discrete and continuous units using whole numbers and fractions in the context of a picnic.

Figure 6.2   Fair sharing at a Teddy Bears' Picnic

Trigger questions

- Is it fair? How do you know?

- What is half of…?

- How can you share equally among the three bears?

- How do you share equally five sandwiches among the three bears?

- How much cake is each of the three bears having?

- If Baby Bear had two plums and the picnic was shared equally, how many plums were there altogether?

Review and reflect

When children have recorded their explanations, play them back to the class and discuss the key mathematical ideas behind fair sharing. Make explicit distinction between continuous units (for example, cake, pie) and discrete units (for example, tomatoes, muffins) and how they can be partitioned equally.

Pay particular attention to the language used by children and make sure they refer to the units being used: for example, Baby Bear is having a third of the whole cake. There are three muffins, so each bear is getting a third of all the muffins, which is one muffin.

In order to emphasize fractions as a quotient, use the sandwiches as the main context and use the question 'how much sandwich is each bear having?' as, if you use 'how many sandwiches', this

(Continued)

(Continued)

question is looking at the additive aspect of the sandwiches rather than the (implicit) multiplicative aspect of fractions. So if there are two sandwiches and three bears, each bear is having two-thirds of all the sandwiches.

Assessment

Children are able to identify the different items to be shared from the picnic whether they are continuous and/or discrete units.

Children use different strategies to share equally such as 'breaking and dealing', halving and repeated halving, dealing with composite units or parallel and radial cutting.

Children use partitioning efficiently and make sure they make equal parts with clear links to the language used to describe fair sharing.

Children start to make judgments such as: 'the more people who come to the picnic, the less I will get'. The more I have to partition one cake (or a given unit) the smaller each part.

Children understand that $2 \div 3 = \frac{2}{3}$.

Follow-up tasks

Children can make up their own picnic stories using different numbers of bears and amounts of food. They can also make 'true/false' stories so other children can find out whether the bears have shared the picnic equally.

ACTIVITY

Shape hunt

Resources

iPads with Numberkiz app installed (available from iTunes store)

Useful links

http://www.exlunch.com/

National curriculum and mathematical understanding links

Suitable for: age 8 and above.

Objectives: to recognize, name and describe 2D shapes in a range of sizes and orientations.

Mathematical understanding: spatial understanding, geometry.

Setting the scene

A shape hunt activity using the school grounds has always been popular in primary schools as it engages children by linking mathematics with the world around them in a meaningful and relevant way. A problem, however, is the way children record the shapes they find around school on the worksheets that are typically used. There is a misplaced emphasis on 'prototype' shapes so when children see a shape in a different orientation, a triangle can become 'an upside triangle'. In other instances, the accuracy with which children record these shapes during the shape hunt does not support their understanding.

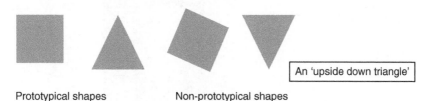

An 'upside down triangle'

Prototypical shapes   Non-prototypical shapes

Figure 6.3   Prototypical and non-prototypical shapes

Start this activity by discussing the two-dimensional shapes in the classroom and then extend the discussion by asking what types of shapes they might find in a shape hunt around the school. Focus the discussion on whether children think they might find regular or irregular polygons and check their understanding of the mathematical vocabulary.

Briefly model the use of the Numberkiz app as the tool that will help children with the shape hunt by taking a picture inside the class.

Home Page   Select the 'plus' sign to add a picture

Figure 6.4   Using the Numberkiz app

On the home page select 'create' and on the following page shown choose the 'plus' sign at the top of the screen. Select picture, then 'camera', take a picture inside the classroom, and model how to use the drawing tools. Discuss the shapes that can be found and identify their properties. Before children go out to the school grounds the teacher may decide to show the main tools children can use to demonstrate the shapes they found. The main tool is the 'line', which will allow children to

(Continued)

(Continued)

trace with their fingers the shapes they can see. An additional tool that this app has in comparison with other similar apps is the option to use some of the shapes commonly used in schools as shown in Figure 6.5.

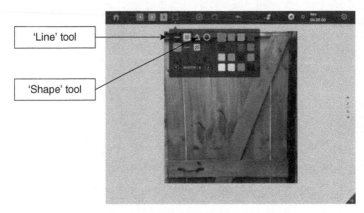

'Line' tool

'Shape' tool

Figure 6.5   Using Numberkiz drawing tools

Let the shape hunt begin. Give children a set amount of time for the hunt so they can find as many polygons as possible. Encourage children to 'spot' irregular shapes, compound shapes and non-prototypical shapes. Ask children to add one picture per slide as this is the default layout of the app.

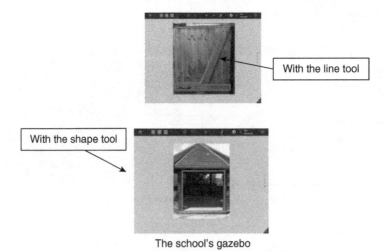

With the line tool

With the shape tool

The school's gazebo

Figure 6.6   Using Numberkiz drawing tools

Once the hunt has finished, children could be asked to take screen shots and post these to the class blog, Google Drive or through Apple Airplay, if available. Another feature that this app offers is the option to record audio in each slide. Simply press record at the top of the page and children can describe the properties of the shape.

Using children's examples, discuss the shapes found and the properties that describe them. Challenge children's possible misconceptions by using non-prototypical shapes and/or irregular quadrilaterals.

Trigger questions

- What is the most interesting shape that you might find? Why?
- What is the same about the shapes you found in the playground? What is different?
- Predict the shapes you are likely to find.
- Have you seen a shape like this before? (Use a non-prototypical shape from children's work.)

Review and reflect

Use children's pictures that have non-prototypical shapes to discuss the properties children can see. Alternatively, use different pictures taken from the same area of the school grounds and compare and describe the shapes found by children.

Use the 'odd one out' strategy to discuss these shapes.

According to children's age and expectations from the curriculum being followed, the children need to discuss the geometric properties of the shapes they have found. These 'properties' refer to the features or attributes of shapes, such as, curved or straight sides, number and equality of angles and sides, symmetry and 'parallelness'.

Some of the key vocabulary that should be used by children includes: regular/irregular polygons; congruence and similarity; reflective/rotational symmetry; equilateral/isosceles/scalene/acute-angled/right-angled/obtuse-angledtrangles;andquadrilaterals(square,rectangle, parallelogram, rhombus, trapezium, kite).

Assessment

The opportunities for assessment are wide depending on the way it was decided to record children's work. If children recorded audio, they can peer assess each other's work by simply swapping iPads between groups. If the teacher is required to show evidence of children's work, ask children to screenshot a picture and label it, which is another feature of the app.

- Describe your shapes to your partner. Can you name them all?
- Can your partner describe their shape using the correct mathematical vocabulary?
- How do you recognize a parallelogram?

Follow-up tasks

- Sort all the shapes you found using a Carroll diagram.
- Using the pictures from the shape hunt, ask children to think about the perimeter and area of the shapes. If children found compound shapes, ask children how they might find the area and perimeter of these shapes.

ACTIVITY

Let's survey!

Resources

Google Forms, laptops, Chrome Books or a table computer

Useful links

- Google Forms: https://www.google.co.uk/forms/about/
- Child Exploitation and Online Protection Centre (CEOP): https://www.thinkuknow.co.uk/
- Childnet International: http://www.childnet.com/
- Template survey: https://goo.gl/yiVz7I

National curriculum and mathematical understanding links

Suitable for: age 9 and above.

Objectives: to be able to collect, represent and interpret data.

Mathematical understanding: statistical understanding and purposeful use of data.

Setting the scene

Surveys in schools have the potential to be very engaging activities if these are closely linked to relevant and meaningful topics for children. These can range from something as simple as 'my favourite pet' in Early Years to more specific topics as part of children's independent projects. The use of Google Forms to carry out surveys allows children to collect, represent and interpret data efficiently.

Before this activity is carried out, children need to have a Google account to access Google Forms. The children may each have a Gmail account or the class teacher may prefer to create one class Gmail account and share the username and password with the class. This decision depends on the class's familiarity with handling email addresses and this will vary across schools. If the class is relatively new to using their own email accounts, it is recommended that in the first instance a single Gmail account is used. Issues of e-safety must be addressed and discussed as a whole class and in accordance with the school's policy. See 'Resources' above for the CEOP and Childnet International websites.

Start the activity by discussing possible questions that children would like to investigate. As this question has to be relevant to children, you might have topics such as, 'How do you travel to school?', in order to help your class environmental champions (or 'green warriors') as part of the school's drive to be environmentally friendly, or as evidence to achieve an environmental award or recognition. An alternative might be a current topic such as the Olympics: for example, 'What is your favourite aquatic sport in the Olympics (Rio 2016 or Tokyo 2020)?'

Log on to Google Drive and create a new Google Form. Start the session by modelling how to create the Google Form in order to gather the data.

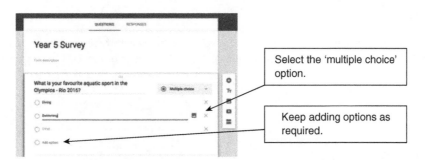

Figure 6.7   Creating a survey using Google Forms

Once all the possible options have been entered, demonstrate how to share the link so children can answer the survey. Click on 'share' and select the link option, which also allows users to shorten the link. Copy the link and email it to the children or post it on the class blog depending on the way the task was originally set up, that is, whether the children have their individual Gmail accounts or are using one account for the whole class.

Figure 6.8   Sharing the link to the survey

Ask the children to answer the survey or have a pre-prepared completed survey. Select 'responses' and show children the results. The default graph used by Google Forms is a pie chart as shown below. Look at the results and discuss the data in order to interpret the data given in the pie chart.

Figure 6.9   Results of the survey using a pie chart

While whole-class discussion continues, encourage children to think about other graphs that will help them to interpret the result further. You can now model how to create a bar graph with the data already collected. While on the 'response' page, click on the 'sheets' icon . This action will create a spreadsheet with all the data collected. Once the spreadsheet has been created,

(Continued)

(Continued)

click on 'insert' and select 'chart', which will display a window with types of graphs as shown in Figure 6.10. Choose the graph you want, click on 'insert' and your graph will be created on your spreadsheet.

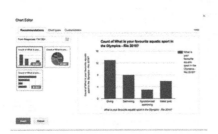 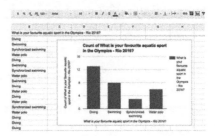

Figure 6.10   Creating a spreadsheet with graphs

Working independently

Children can now create their own surveys related to a topic agreed beforehand or perhaps as part of their independent projects. As a mini plenary, use one of the children's graphs and ask them to interpret the data with their partners. Then ask children to create their own questions for you to collate. Once children have the results, ask them to share the results and say whether the original question has been answered.

Trigger questions

- What is the most popular response?
- What is the least popular response?
- Did your survey answer your question?
- Will your results be the same across the school? Yes or no? Why?
- What is the difference between …?
- Do you think your results are representative across the year group/school?
- If you repeated the survey, would you get the same or different results? Why?

Review and reflect

A starting point is to ask children the same question for all the different surveys they carried out: 'What is the most/least popular response?'

One of the key areas that children need to understand is the possible limitations of the data and therefore the interpretation. Discuss the size of the sample and how representative it might/ might not be. Will the results of their survey be similar in another school in the local area? Discuss whether asking different groups of people might give different results, and why this might be the case.

Assessment

Children are able to interpret the data.

Was your collection of data accurate? How do you know?

Did you find out the answer to your original question?

Did your choice of graph help you interpret the data?

Is there anything surprising about your results? If yes, why that might be?

Follow-up tasks

- As a class, devise some questions that could apply to all types of surveys and then questions that might be only specific to the children's individual surveys.
- Write a short blog entry to present your results.
- Look at cross-curricular links with non-fiction writing using evidence from data. See Chapter 12 on the historical and cultural roots of mathematics to discover how Florence Nightingale used data to make a strong case for better hygiene during the Crimean war.

WEBSITES, WEBSITES...

The choice of educational websites is overwhelming, but the following are particularly useful in the teaching of mathematics as they have either been designed as part of research projects or are able to model mathematical concepts effectively.

FRACTIONS LAB HTTP://FRACTIONSLAB.LKL.AC.UK/

Fractions Lab has two main components that make it a very powerful resource to help children develop a deep conceptual understanding of fractions. The first feature is its ability to represent fractions using linear, area, set and capacity models. The second feature is that the user can then compare fractions or add and subtract fractions. These operations are carried out using the representations generated on the interactive environment provided, which avoids the use of procedures being taught to children without their understanding.

ILLUMINATIONS HTTPS://ILLUMINATIONS.NCTM.ORG/ GAMES-PUZZLES.ASPX

This has a very good range of interactive resources that can be used to model several mathematical concepts as a whole class. For example: Algebra Tiles, Fraction Models or Geometric Solids. Other resources can be used as independent, group tasks or games such as: Deep Sea Duel, Factor Game, Concentration or Primary Krypto.

PLICKERS (APP AVAILABLE FROM ITUNES STORE)

Plickers is not restricted to mathematics teaching but its usefulness resides in the easy and fast way it identifies how children's understanding is progressing within or at the end of a lesson. In mathematics teaching, it is crucial to identify misconceptions as efficiently as possible so that teaching can be adapted to address any misconceptions as they arise. Plickers allows teachers to use 'low-stakes' assessment through the use of multiple-choice or true/false quizzes. See Figure 6.11 for an example of a multiple choice question using pictures or photos.

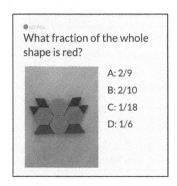

Figure 6.11   Example of a multiple choice quiz question using Plickers

REFERENCES

BeCTA (2009) *Primary Mathematics and ICT: a pupil's entitlement to ICT in primary mathematics*, https://www.stem.org.uk/system/files/elibrary-resources/legacy_files_migrated/13809-entitlement_maths.pdf.

Behr, MJ, Harel, G, Post, T and **Lesh, R** (1992) 'Rational number, ratio, and proportion', in D. Grouws (ed.), *Handbook of Research on Mathematics Teaching and Learning*. New York: Macmillan, pp. 296–333.

Clark-Wilson, A, Aldon, G, Cusi, A, Goos, M, Haspekian, M, Robutti, O and **Thomas, MOJ** (2014) 'The challenges of teaching mathematics with digital technologies – the evolving role of the teacher', in Liljedahl, P, Nichol, C, Oesterle, S and Allan, D (eds) *Proceedings of the Joint Meeting of PME 38 and PME-NA 36*. Vancouver: PME, pp. 87–116.

Gillen, J and **Barton, D** (2010) *Digital Literacies. A Research Briefing by the Technology Enhanced Learning Phase of the Teaching and Learning Research Programme*. London Knowledge Lab, Institute of Education.

Lamon, SJ (2007) 'Rational numbers and proportional reasoning: toward a theoretical framework for research', in F Lester (ed.), *Second Handbook of Research on Mathematics Teaching and Learning*, NC: Information Age Publishing, pp. 629–67.

Noss, R, Cox, R, Laurillard, D, Luckin, R, Plowman, L, Scanlon, E and **Sharples, M** (2012) 'System upgrade: realising the vision for UK education', *American Journal of Engineering Research*, 5(12): 313–17.

Nunes, T and **Bryant, P** (2009) 'Understanding rational numbers and intensive quantities', in T Nunes, P Bryant and A Wilson (eds), Key Understandings in Mathematics Learning. University of Oxford: Nuffield Foundation.

7

GAMES FOR LEARNING MATHEMATICS

RAY HUNTLEY

─────── IN THIS CHAPTER ───────

This chapter:

- demonstrates how games can enrich learning
- considers the features of games that are useful in learning
- supports the design of your own games for learning and teaching mathematics
- considers how to assess the learning that has taken place.

Many people have memories of mathematics as difficult to learn and lessons not being much fun. Learning mathematics should be challenging, but there is no reason why it should not be enjoyable. One way to do this is to learn skills and concepts through playing games. Children have always enjoyed playing games of all kinds, and games in mathematics can enrich learning. As teachers, we can use mathematical games as part of our planned provision to increase engagement with mathematics. The same games can be used at home to reinforce learning. In this chapter, I set out the benefits of different games in mathematics lessons, explore a range of different types of games and provide ways of designing and evaluating new games to optimize mathematical outcomes. This will help you be more aware of the value of using games for mathematics learning.

We can conceive of a game as a situation where two or more 'players' are competing to achieve a predetermined winning situation, perhaps scoring points, or placing pieces in a position so the opponent cannot continue. Chess would come into this category, for example. In any game, however, it is perhaps best to insist that the players are trying to 'win' through their own efforts, thoughts, decisions and actions, rather than relying on 'chance' alone as in, for example, a game such as Snakes and Ladders. Obviously, many games involve both 'chance' and decisions such as Ludo, Backgammon and Monopoly.

The key features of a game, whether mathematical or not, are:

- an element of challenge, either a player trying to achieve an outcome for themselves, but more often against an opponent

- a set of rules that determine how the game is to be played

- an end point or winning position.

How can these elements be integrated into a game that can benefit children's mathematical learning?

There are many aspects of learning that can be enhanced through using mathematical games. The first is motivation. Children enjoy playing games, and if they are offered a game to play, they may not at first see the mathematics within it, but will no doubt be motivated to play, seeing a game as something fun, rather than 'work'. This can increase a child's self-esteem, which can help improve their confidence and develop a positive attitude towards mathematics. Losing a game or not scoring as many points as you hoped might be disappointing, but children accept this as part and parcel of games, and this helps avoid a sense of failure at mathematics which, once started, can be very hard to stop or reverse. Being motivated to play, gives children a sense of independence and means that you do not have to be checking that the child is 'on task' as much as in more traditional classroom work.

By using games for mathematics, you can ensure focused outcomes are achieved that relate to specific learning objectives. These could be, for instance, the development of specific number skills, or recognition of shape properties, encountered and developed through the careful selection of particular games that provide realistic and meaningful contexts. This is further beneficial as you can align the game and its outcomes with assessment opportunities arising from the child playing that game, particularly if the child's 'moves' or decisions during the game are recorded in some way or observed by an adult.

Because games can be varied in terms of their challenge and context, you can vary the level of challenge in the game and adapt it to suit the needs of different groups of children. Even within a given game, different children could be experiencing different learning due to their prior experience and attainment. The use of games can enhance learning since they allow for much greater interaction between children, and due to the nature of games, there is an increased level of problem solving already built into the game, even from the perspective of solving the problem 'how do I win this game?' The games that follow are all designed to offer a problem-solving context in a fun and competitive situation.

DESIGNING GAMES

While there is a plethora of ready-made games, old and new, from various cultures, some need to be adapted if they are to help develop specific mathematics skills. New games can be developed from existing games to suit a specific learning purpose, or they can be devised by children. In the games suggested below, some possible variations are proposed that change the particulars of a game without necessarily altering the rules and aims of the game. Beyond this kind of adaptation, it is possible to design new games using some simple approaches.

One such approach is to change the components used in a game while adhering to the basic rules, but with more specific mathematical content. For example, instead of playing dominos with the standard set, make a set of dominos where each end of the domino has a number represented in some way, perhaps as a numeral, or an arrangement of spots, or as the result of a calculation. They can then be played in the usual way, building a chain of dominos by matching the ends together that show the equivalent number.

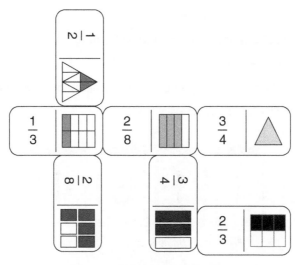

Figure 7.1   Mathematical dominos

Another approach is to take an existing board game and replace the rules and instructions with mathematical problems or tasks. For example, when moving pieces around a Ludo board, there could be mathematics questions at particular positions that the player must answer when they land on that position. When playing Monopoly, there could be additional 'chance' or 'community chest' cards that set a mathematical challenge.

One of the most effective and enjoyable ways to design new games is to allow groups of children to design their own game (see Shell Centre materials in 'References' at the end of this chapter). They can be guided towards having a particular theme, perhaps linked to something they are studying in other curriculum areas, and helped to make decisions about the number of players, type of board or playing environment to use and to include some mathematics that can be done while playing the game. Children are very creative and enjoy designing boards for games, and various playing pieces, cards, rules and scoring systems. Of course, time is needed to develop, make and test new games, but the motivation and focus is well worth it.

As well as the learning that goes on during the design and make phase, and the fun of playing the game, it is useful to get the children to evaluate their game according to a set of agreed criteria. For example: can it be played by different age groups, does it include strategy, or chance, or both, and is it an enjoyable or frustrating game to play? These are important questions in determining the effectiveness of a game so that it encourages others to want to play and feel they have a chance of winning, as well as achieving the mathematical objectives that it set out to meet. Of course, the best games are those that children want to take home and play.

ACTIVITY

24 Game

Resources

This game requires nothing more than pencil and paper, although a set of playing cards without the 10, Jack, Queen, King can also be used, or a prepared set of cards with single digits, four each of all the numerals 1 to 9.

National curriculum and mathematical understanding links

Suitable for: age 8 and above.

Objectives: to combine four single digits using arithmetical operations to achieve a total of 24.

Mathematical understanding: calculation skills.

Figure 7.2   Number cards for 24 Game

Setting the scene

The game can be introduced by looking at an example of the number game from the TV show 'Countdown', where the contestants choose several numbers and then have to make a given total.

This game is always played using four numbers and the answer must always be 24. The numbers can be randomly issued or given from a pre-determined list of known solutions that can be targeted according to the players. Some number combinations are more difficult to find a solution than others, for example, 3, 3, 8, 8 is particularly challenging for making 24.

Trigger questions

- How can we make 24 using the four numbers?
- Can we make this in different ways?

Review and reflect

Have you used all four numbers?

Have you made the total 24?

Have you used the arithmetic operations correctly?

Assessment

Children can ask each other the review and reflect questions to ensure they have done the task correctly.

Follow-up tasks

While the game is designed to be played with four numbers to make 24, this can obviously be varied, using fewer or more numbers and setting the target to be different values. One popular version is to use four of the same number and see which numbers from 1 to 20 can be made. Or you can use the digits of the current year to make every number possible from 1 to 20. This is rather limited in the current century while one of the digits is zero.

ACTIVITY

Strike it Out!

Resources

This game requires use of a number line, either drawn out to cross numbers off, or in a form where counters can be placed on the used numbers.

Useful links

This game is one of many excellent activities available freely from the NRICH website (www.nrich. maths.org/6589)

National curriculum and mathematical understanding links

Suitable for: age 5 and above

Objectives: mental mathematics, recording calculations, developing strategy.

```
Number Line
0 1 2 3 4 5 6 7 8 9 10 11 12 13 14 15 16 17 18 19 20
```

Figure 7.3   Number line for Strike it Out

Setting the scene

Introduce the game by displaying a number line and asking children to form a calculation using three numbers from the number line. To start with, you may want to restrict children to using

(Continued)

(Continued)

either addition or subtraction. Select one of the calculations, for example, $4 + 3 = 7$. In the next turn, children have to make a number sentence that starts with the previous answer, so $7 + 11 = 18$ is a possibility. The game continues with each new calculation starting with the previous answer, using only numbers that have not yet been used. As the numbers get used up, it becomes harder to make a calculation. When one child cannot make a number sentence with the numbers left, they have lost the game.

Trigger questions

Once several numbers are used up, the teacher might ask children to look more carefully for number sentences, perhaps focusing more on numbers close together, or answers that are either large or small.

Review and reflect

The review of the game will be to identify whether any number sentences can be made using the remaining numbers on the number line. Older children might then begin to think about strategies to ensure they can win the game.

Assessment

Children can be involved in self-peer assessment by asking each other why they selected particular number sentences when more than one option was possible, and whether an alternative choice might have changed the game outcome.

Follow-up tasks

The game can be varied according to the set of numbers and the operations used. For example, should it go from 0-10? 1-10? 0-20? 0-30? Does it make a difference if zero is included?

An interesting alternative to this game (which could be deployed in other strategy games) is to move from playing competitively and trying to beat the opponent, to playing collaboratively, and together trying to use up as many numbers as possible. It can be reasoned that it is not possible to use every number on a 1-20 line, since the first sentence uses three numbers, leaving 17, and each new sentence uses another two numbers, always leaving an odd number to be used.

ACTIVITY

Turkeys

National curriculum and mathematical understanding links

Suitable for: age 9 and above.

Objectives: this game requires spatial awareness and some logical strategic thinking.

Turkeys is a game played on a four-by-four grid. It requires two players, one of whom is the turkey and one is the farmer. The turkey is a counter of one colour that starts in a corner of the grid, and the farmer has two counters, starting on two adjacent corners of the grid, as shown in Figure 7.4.

The turkey has to try to avoid being captured by the farmer, by moving the counter one square in any direction. The farmer must try to catch the turkey by surrounding the turkey with the two counters in a linear arrangement, one either side of the turkey either vertically or horizontally. On each turn, the farmer can only move one counter, one square in any direction.

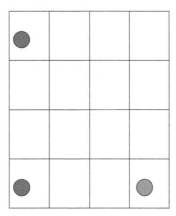

Figure 7.4   Grid for Turkeys game

Setting the scene

This game could be introduced using any of a number of stories based on farmyard settings, or where farmers are trying to round up missing stock. For children who have played draughts or chess, there will be some familiarity with board games that require pieces to be moved in certain directions, and the notion of being captured.

The game has different strategies for each player, given their respective aims and the different number of counters they each have. It is an interesting exercise to identify which areas of the board are 'safe' for the turkey, and how the farmer can manage to trap the turkey. To avoid endless play where the turkey keeps running from the farmer, it can be specified that the farmer wins when the turkey is caught, but if the turkey manages 20 moves without being caught, then the turkey has won.

Trigger questions

- What is the best strategy for the turkey?
- What is the best strategy for the farmer?
- Are there any safe squares for the turkey?
- Which squares should the farmer aim for?

(Continued)

(Continued)

Review and reflect

The review of this game is likely to be best served by revisiting the trigger questions once the children have played the game on a number of occasions and have become familiar with it.

Assessment

Children can be encouraged to discuss their strategies and reflect on how well they are able to apply them.

Follow-up tasks

Vary this game by changing the grid size, or maybe giving the farmer three counters, or change how many moves the turkey has to avoid capture.

ACTIVITY

21

National curriculum and mathematical understanding links

Suitable for: age 6 and above.

Objectives: to count alternately in steps of one, two or three with the aim of being the person to reach 21.

Mathematical understanding: counting skills and reasoning to determine how to reach 21.

The game '21' is about number strategy and relies on nothing more complicated than counting. In a typical version, two players take turns to count, successively counting from one up to 21, each person is allowed to add one, two or three numbers to the count. The winner is the player who gets to complete the count on 21. A typical game might proceed as follows, with the players counting denoted by bold and italic type respectively:

1, 2, ...*3, 4, 5,* ...**6,** ...*7, 8,* ...**9, 10, 11,** ...*12, 13, 14,* ...**15,** ...*16, 17,* ...**18,** ...*19, 20, 21.*

This game leads very quickly to a recursive strategy, whereby it becomes apparent that to get to 21, first you need to get to 17, but to get to 17 you must first get to 13, and so on.

Setting the scene

The game can be introduced by counting up and back from zero to various numbers, perhaps 20, which can be reached by counting in steps of 1, 2, 4, 5 or 10. This can lead to discussion about which equal counting steps can get to a given number. The game can be seen firstly as ways of counting in equal steps to 21, which of course can be reached in 7 steps of 3, but then the challenge comes in being able to choose unequal steps of 1, 2 or 3 and seeking to be the person who reaches 21.

Trigger questions

- How can we count up to 21 in equal steps?
- Can we do this in different ways?

Review and reflect

- Did you reach 21 before your playing partner?
- Did you always jump correctly, that is, in jumps of one, two or three?
- When did you know you would be able to reach 21?

Assessment

Children can ask each other the review and reflect questions to ensure they have done the task correctly.

Follow-up tasks

While the game is designed to be played counting to 21, this can obviously be varied, using a smaller or larger target number and setting the jump size to be different amounts.

ACTIVITY

Nim

National curriculum and mathematical understanding links

Suitable for: age 9 and above.

Objectives: to reason and think strategically to reduce a set of objects to leave the last object for a playing partner.

Nim can take various forms, but in each version, the aim is to reduce a number of piles or rows of counters until just one counter remains. This is effectively a special version of the '21' game described earlier. The version described here involves a starting arrangement of five rows of counters (matchsticks, buttons, or tally marks on paper can also be used), with a row of five, then four, then three, two and one. It is important to keep the counters in each row together, and to ensure that

(Continued)

(Continued)

the rows remain distinct. The starting arrangement is shown in Figure 7.5. Each player then takes turns in choosing a row and removing as many counters as they wish from that row. Play continues until there is a single counter remaining. The player who is left with this counter is the loser.

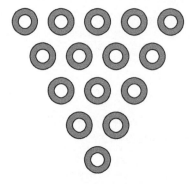

Figure 7.5   Triangular layout for Nim game

This game quickly allows players to develop strategies based on pattern recognition and reasoning. The thought processes involved in playing will often lead to questions such as 'What if I take that, what will they do?', or 'What if they take those, what can I do?' and such questions, starting with 'what if?' are very useful in all mathematics for developing reasoning and problem solving.

Setting the scene

The game can be introduced by arranging 15 items in the triangular layout as shown and once the rules are explained, allow children time to play and gain experience in how to play and begin to develop strategies that they think will result in a win.

Trigger questions

- Which row should you take from first?
- How many objects should you take on each turn?
- Is there a pattern to ensure you win?

Review and reflect

- Were you able to plan a way of winning?
- Did you discover any patterns?

Assessment

Children can discuss the game collaboratively and identify whether they did the best move or whether they should have taken a different set of objects on their move.

Follow-up tasks

Another version of Nim starts with three piles instead of five rows, and each pile can have any number of counters, but essentially the strategies are similar. The underlying mathematics relies on an understanding of binary arithmetic and is described nicely in Martin Gardner's *Mathematical Puzzles and Diversions*. Here, Gardner (1975) outlines how to 'calculate' a safe winning position in any form of Nim.

ACTIVITY

Replicating sports with dice

Resources

This activity requires the use of many dice, generally the standard 1-6 version, but others could also be used.

It can be immensely rewarding to design a game that can be played with dice or spinners in which the numbers generated can act as scores for a selected sport. Dice cricket has been a popular pastime for many fans over the years, with ready-made kits available to buy online.

Useful links

Information and news about sports results are readily available on the internet.

National curriculum and mathematical understanding links

Suitable for: age 10 and above.

Objectives: to simulate a real-life sport using the random outcomes of dice. In such a simulation, notions of probability are explored.

Figure 7.6   Dice

(Continued)

(Continued)

Setting the scene

Dice football exists in various forms, but it is a nice mathematical challenge to try to design a version where the match scores are replicated using dice (see Figure 7.6, p. 119), to achieve realistic scores that can be used to play a series of knockout matches or a league format. While some commercial versions exist, they are complicated, and it is always best to keep things simple. One version can be played using three dice as follows:

- Team 1 rolls three dice for the first half score: 6 is a goal, 4 or 5 is a 'half goal'.

- Team 2 then rolls three dice for their first half score: only 6 counts as a goal.

- Team 1 rolls three dice for their second half score: 6 is a goal, 5 is a 'half goal'.

- Finally, Team 2 rolls three dice for their second half score: only 6 counts as a goal.

This format produces realistic scores to actual football matches. It also builds in 'home' advantage for Team 1, with half-goals only counting if they pair up to make complete goals over the two halves of the match. The downside of this system is that it tends to lead to fewer high-scoring matches than occur in real football.

Trigger questions

- How can we use the random numbers on a dice to generate realistic football scores?

- Can we do this with different numbers or types of dice?

- Can we apply this idea to other sports?

Review and reflect

- Have you created a way of getting realistic scores?

- Can you compare your dice-generated result with a real set of football results, for example as found online or in a newspaper?

- How can you improve your system?

Assessment

Children can ask each other the review and reflect questions to ensure they have done the task correctly.

Follow-up tasks

While the task is to try to generate realistic scores, some children may find it sufficiently challenging to generate scores that can be used as the basis of a competition. It is unlikely that a score of 6–4 will occur in real football, but it does at least generate a winner and loser. This can be used to introduce the ideas of round-robin league tournaments and knockout competitions, which can lead to understanding how results and league tables are formed, and an understanding of how knockout tournaments are based on having a number of competitors that is equal to a power of 2, that is, 2, 4, 8, 16, 32, and so on.

GAMES FROM AROUND THE WORLD

Humans have played games throughout the ages. Many museums have games from Africa, the ancient Romans and so on. Children could work in small groups to find an ancient game, figure out how it works and then teach others in the class.

REFERENCES

Gardner, M (1975) *Mathematical Puzzles and Diversions*. London: Penguin Books.

Shell Centre for Mathematical Education Publications (1987). *Design a Board Game*. Available at: http://www.mathshell.com/materials.php?series=numeracy&item=boardgame

FURTHER READING

Gardner, M (1977) *Mathematical Carnival*. New York: Vintage Books.

8

USING AND DEVELOPING MATHEMATICS SKILLS ACROSS THE CURRICULUM

KAREN WILDING

IN THIS CHAPTER

This chapter:

- explores how mathematics can be taught across the curriculum
- highlights the importance of real-life context for children
- helps you to recognize the potential of everyday things like the weather forecast for the learning and teaching of mathematics.

MATHEMATICS IN THE NEWS!

Too many mathematics lessons begin with abstract recording of symbols and procedures where the actual mathematics involved is totally divorced from any real relevance and meaning for the learner. Teaching in this way leads many children to believe that mathematics happens in a classroom and on paper rather than in real life as a powerful tool to solve many of life's intriguing problems.

The activities in this chapter aim to address the need to embed learning in meaning and show children why developing their thinking and ability to work mathematically is not only crucial to life but also extremely enjoyable.

As Boaler (2008) describes, the time for change is now:

> In many classrooms, a very narrow subject is taught to children, that is nothing like the maths of the world or the maths that mathematicians use. This narrow subject involves copying methods that teachers demonstrate and reproducing them accurately, over and over again. But this narrow subject is not mathematics, it is a strange mutated version of the subject that is taught in our schools. When the real mathematics is taught instead – the whole subject that involves problem solving, creating ideas and representations, exploring puzzles, discussing methods and many different ways of working – then many more people are successful. This is the classic 'win win' situation – teaching real maths, means teaching the authentic version of the subject and giving children a taste of high level mathematical work; it also means that many more children will be successful in school and in life.

There is a rich potential for mathematics within every newspaper, a free and plentiful resource that connects to everyday life. The activities introduce some of the many ways we can use the mathematics in newspapers as starting points for problem solving in everyday contexts.

The first activity is suitable for children in the Early Years and for those beginning Key Stage 1. Extensions are then given to develop the same starting point through Key Stage 1 and into Key Stage 2. I recommend you read through all the activities before selecting what is most suitable for your learners. Careful consideration needs to be given at every key stage regarding children's familiarity with newspapers; in our digital world many children may have very limited hands-on experience to draw upon and will need time to explore the resource freely at first. There are also considerable cross-curricular opportunities with such a wide resource.

ACTIVITY

Number hunt!

National curriculum and mathematical understanding links

Suitable for: Early Years and Key Stage 1

Objectives: to recognize numerals and numbers; to distinguish numerals and numbers from letters; to read and make sense of numbers in context; opportunities to talk about magnitude of numbers; to build and order numbers; development of place value.

Setting the scene

Always check the content carefully (text and images) before using newspapers in class and judge their suitability for the children who will be using them.

(Continued)

(Continued)

Allow the children time to look through the newspapers first. It is easy to assume that children are familiar with such an everyday item but many may not be and need time to explore, notice, question and discuss what they see.

Introducing the activity using an engagement factor, 'hook'

Share with the children that they are going to be mathematics detectives and go on a number hunt. As they go about searching for numbers in the newspapers, encourage their noticing skills and place emphasis upon talking to each other about what they see and how they know it is a number.

Get children to work in pairs to find numbers in the newspaper. These could be cut out or copied. Distinguishing between digits and letters is something younger children are learning to do and the range of sizes, font styles, colours, etc. helps them begin to understand the many ways digits can be written.

Children will discover examples where digits are combined to create different numbers, for example, 'Here is a 1 and a 2 and it says 12', and also where digits are used in their 'nominal' sense, for example, for a bar code or phone number where they remain a series of digits and are read as such rather than representing a number with cardinal and ordinal value.

Trigger questions

- Were there any numbers we found a lot of? This may open up a discussion about 'numbers' that are actually digits being combined to create numbers. Are children aware that the same digits are used repeatedly for numbers of any size?

- Can you find the same number written differently? How many numbers like this can you find?

- Can you find numbers that are written bigger and smaller? This may lead to some interesting discussions among Early Years children about 'big' numbers and 'little' numbers.

Review and assessment

The following questions are intended to be used for effective formative assessment. Give the children time to talk together. Adults need to listen, gather and capture what is heard, and avoid correcting or extending children's explanations with their understanding. Instead, adults can note down on the board what children say and use the notes to show interest in their thinking processes. Use what is gathered to reflect upon and plan your next steps.

- Are there a lot of numbers in newspapers?

- What digits did we notice in our numbers? What numbers did the digits make?

- Were there any numbers where we knew the digits but did not know how to read the number?

- Are some of your numbers 'bigger' than others? How do you know?

- Did you notice anything else about the numbers that you could share with us?

ACTIVITY

Investigating the role of numbers

National curriculum and mathematical understanding links

This activity is an extension of 'Number hunt' above.

Suitable for: Key Stages 1 and 2

Mathematics skills: reasoning about numbers in context; using conjecture to determine role of numbers; and developing an understanding of how signs and abbreviations are used widely in mathematics to express meaning.

Setting the scene

Introduce the activity as 'Number detectives' and emphasize the need for careful looking, noticing and discussion (rather than speed and 'right' answers!).

Introducing the activity using an engagement factor, 'hook'

Ask the children to hunt for numbers and record them but also notice how the number is being used, for example, as a page number, price, etc.

Be careful not to make any suggestions at this early stage as to what these might be but instead allow the children to begin investigating and then listen in and capture what they are saying.

Pause the activity when the children have begun to discuss what they see and you have had the opportunity (perhaps after five to ten minutes) to assess where they are with their thinking. Plan questions that build directly upon what you have seen to deepen their exploration. Encourage them to notice but do not tell them *what* to notice.

Gather what they are discussing and display on the board. Examples from the children might include:

- Is it the price of the paper?
- Is it the date?
- Is it the page number?
- Is it a temperature?
- Is it a time?
- Is it an amount of money?
- It is a number of people?
- Is it a special offer?
- Is it a percentage?

(Continued)

(Continued)

Children can be asked to extend their thinking by finding examples that look like 'numbers' but are actually only *lists of digits*, for example, phone numbers, bar codes, bus numbers, road numbers, etc. Confusingly, these are almost always referred to as 'numbers' but actually have no numeric value and are being used in the 'nominal' form as labels.

Review and assessment

Capture a range of numbers the children have found as you circulate the class.

Capture a list of labels and abbreviations the children have found, for example, £, p, kg, m, °, %.

Write these up on the board and ask the children to discuss whether there are any numbers that are unlikely to be coupled with one of the labels and reason why. For example, there might be 278,500 for a house price? What would your reasoning be?

ACTIVITY

Confusing labels?

This activity is a further extension of 'Number hunt' above.

Numbers are often accompanied by letters and symbols, for example, km, %, £, kg, m (meaning million as well as metre).

These letters and symbols are another way of understanding how numbers are being used and what the person using them means to communicate. It can be very confusing, so investigating and researching their meanings, and whether any have more than one meaning, is a very valuable learning experience.

National curriculum and mathematical understanding links

Suitable for: Key Stage 2

Mathematics skills: reasoning around and applying understanding of place value and consistent use of groups of ten (leading to tenths, hundredths, etc.) in money and measures, for example, mass, length, temperature; making sense of concepts such as percentages in context before specific mathematics skills are taught in depth.

Introducing the activity using an engagement factor, 'hook'

Introduce this activity by offering children the opportunity to experience similar tasks to the above at a 'stage appropriate' level. For example, you could place emphasis upon ordering the numbers found in the first activity, sorting according to properties (multiples of, odd numbers, factors, etc.). It is important to allow children to explore the resource and become familiar with a newspaper's layout and style.

Trigger questions

Allow time to notice and collect these symbols alongside the numbers they accompany before asking:

- If I saw 12m in the newspaper what might the 'm' mean?
- If the story was about the cost of a new road what symbols might we expect and why?
- If the story was about an anaconda what symbols might we expect and why?

When we take account of context, numbers' meanings can change dramatically. If the 'm' is 'million', how could the number '12m' have been written and why has the writer chosen to write '12m' instead?

Exploring consistent number relationships and use of language to support reasoning

Although numbers have different meanings in different contexts, tasks such as these offer opportunities to explore, when we look at the numbers themselves, how we find the same mathematical relationships occurring. For example, when we read an article about the length of something, we can reason that 1.27m means '1 whole metre and 27 centimetres'. We can then work explicitly in 'Maths World' to understand that we have 'one whole metre' and the use of the decimal point tells us we have part of another metre but not a whole one. This metre has been split into ten equal parts and we have two of these parts: 1.27. These tenths have also been divided into ten equal parts and we have seven of these: 1.27. So we can now reason that the first digit after the decimal point stands for tenths of a metre and the second digit for hundredths of a metre.

All of this exploration is best carried out while looking at a metre stick and/or tape measure, which will help to make the concept far more accessible to all children.

Developing understanding using 'concrete' apparatus

Building models of these relationships using Dienes (base ten) equipment allows children to then generalize further and see that this relationship exists within other measurement contexts including money.

For example, 1.27l represents 1 whole litre, 2 tenths of a litre and 7 hundredths of a litre. The 'base ten' model remains exactly the same but this time the 'unit' we are working in is litres. The Latin language we use can be extremely helpful here: 'decilitres' with 'deci-' meaning 'tenth', and 'centilitres' with 'centi' meaning 'hundredth'. Naturally, if we then divide our hundred into ten parts, we will have created a thousand parts of a litre, hence 'millilitre' with 'milli' meaning 'thousandth'.

Transferring understanding and generalizing

When children begin to reason that the 2 in 1.27 represents 2 tenths, the 7 in 1.27 represents 7 hundredths of the unit and they have built models to help them notice, manipulate and understand this relationship, they should be encouraged to see that the '27' in 1.27 could also be seen

(Continued)

(Continued)

as '27 hundredths'. This knowledge becomes particularly useful when dealing with money and understanding that in '£1.27' the '2' represents '2 tenths' of the whole pound and the 7 represents '7 hundredths' of the pound and could be made using 20p + 7p (5p + 2p) but we could also see 27p as 27 pennies. If there are 100 pennies in a pound then we can reason that in £1.27 the '27' represents '27 hundredths' of the unit.

Cross-curricular links

Link the study of 'Romans' in history with children's growing awareness of how many Latin words are used in mathematics. When we know 'deci', 'centi' and 'milli', we can use the names of measures to help us reason about mathematical relationships. Many other words in mathematics derive from Greek origins, for example, 'kilo', and 'gon' as in 'pentagon' from the Greek 'gonia' meaning 'knee (angle)'.

Extension and variation

This learning could easily be extended away from newspapers into recipes where children learn to interpret and reason about relationships and the etymology of 'kg', 'g', 'ml', 'l', etc. Without the life experience that as adults we often take for granted, these letters and the quantities and relationships they represent are not at all obvious to children. When we allow time for exploration, talk and children's own explanations and generalizations then many essential mathematical connections can be made.

Assessment and review

Challenge the children to go home and photograph many examples of numbers with labels or abbreviations and reason what they mean.

Create a class quiz-style activity where the other children try to work out where at home they might find this number written in this way.

Are there ways we could give a clue but not all of the information? For example, the display on a dishwasher might say 137 and have no label but we could work out where the picture was taken and therefore what it was communicating (an excellent example for working in groups of 60 (for minutes) and not 100).

ACTIVITY

Weather watch

Weather is one of the easiest and most meaningful mathematical contexts to bring into our classrooms at every stage of the Primary Years learning journey. We all experience the weather on a day-to-day basis and, as we know, our conversations often centre around it.

Useful links

Meteorological (met) office website: http://www.metoffice.gov.uk/; http://www.metoffice.gov.uk/learning/weather-for-schools

National curriculum and mathematical understanding links

Suitable for: all year groups

Mathematics skills: collecting and interpreting meaningful data; reading, building, drawing, interpreting and comparing decimal value; developing reasoning through exploring and building models; creating mathematical drawings of 'greater than', 'less than' and 'difference' within a meaningful context; calculating using known facts relating to 'ten' and place value.

This activity is ideal as an ongoing, increasingly challenging use of number in context, and use and interpretation of statistics

Noticing

One of the greatest skills children can be encouraged to use and develop is that of noticing. Awareness of our surroundings feeds our curiosity of the world and a desire to make sense of our experiences. This curiosity and innate drive to *problem solve* is the essential foundation for all mathematical learning.

Setting the scene

Invest in thermometers for inside and outside the classroom. Traditional thermometers have a scale that can be very helpful for helping children to relate different types of weather to different temperatures.

Digital thermometers, which have probes that can be placed in different places and use 'wireless' technology, are now very affordable and reflect the effective use of available technology in the digital age our children are growing up in.

Introducing the activity using an engagement factor, 'hook'

Take the class outside at different times of the day to notice how the temperature feels. Discuss how their skin feels and what they are wearing. It is important that children connect the thermometer reading with their own ability to judge temperature and detect changes during the day. This helps give mathematics real meaning.

Show the children clips from the weather forecast online and encourage them to watch it and look for this information elsewhere when they are at home.

Show them the meteorological (met) office website and explain how information and data about weather all around the world is constantly gathered, and how computers are used to help determine what the weather is likely to be every day. Help the children to begin to see that meteorology relies upon mathematics to predict the weather.

(Continued)

(Continued)

Cross-curricular links

This activity has cross-curricular links in geography for which children study their local environment, develop field study skills, and study climate change around, the world, including specific aspects such as 'The Water Cycle'.

Trigger questions

- What have you noticed about the temperature at different times of year?
- What might we expect to 'read' on the thermometer when it is cold enough to need a coat, or warm enough to want to swim outside?
- How does the temperature change during the day? What are your ideas about this and why?
- Is it the same temperature all over the UK as it is here? Why might it be different and where might it be colder or warmer?

Use maps of the UK, including met office satellite images to bring this discussion to life and create cross-curricular links.

What is the weather like in different countries that we know about? How might the weather affect temperatures? Can it be dry and cold? Hot and wet? Are some places very cold at night and hot during the day? Are some places very sunny but cold?

Follow-up tasks

Teach the children to take readings during the day both inside and outside the classroom. Link to the clothes we choose to wear, how our fridge feels (less than 5°C – a useful and accessible reference point), etc.

Build interlocking cubes to show daily temperatures (see Figure 8.1). Use two colours only (to represent hot and cold) and group cubes into tens so that children are encouraged to use their place value and subitizing skills rather than counting in ones.

Figure 8.1   Interlocking cubes showing temperatures over five consecutive days

Label the cubes with the days of the week, indoor/outdoor, and the time of day if taking more than one reading (ideal for older children's investigations).

Predict any change in temperature before readings are taken using our noticing skills and ability to feel temperature.

Notice how temperatures are changing daily and interpret this using appropriate vocabulary: for example, the temperature is increasing or decreasing, it feels warmer/cooler.

Does the temperature going up mean it feels warm? For example, it was 6°C yesterday and today it is 8°C. Does this mean that it feels warm?

Notice when temperatures are equal, approximately equal and very different, and use this to explore the meaningful use of signs such as = ≈ (approximately equal) > < ≠ (not equal). When understood and used in context, these signs are highly appropriate for the youngest children to use and learn that mathematics symbols are an alternative to written words as a means of communication.

Use the concrete representations of temperature to ask questions that develop children's understanding of 'difference'. Transfer the concrete model to a vertical number line to show how we can record what we see.

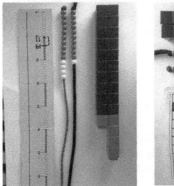 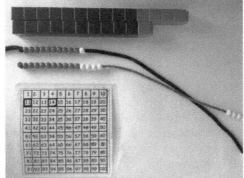

Figure 8.2 Connecting models of 'difference' using concrete and pictorial/symbolic recording

Exploring the concept of 'average'

When children watch or listen to a weather forecast, they will often hear the word 'average' used with regards to temperature, rainfall, etc. Using the interlocking cubes, we can easily explore the earliest stages of the concept of 'mean' average by looking at ways to make each temperature across our data as 'equal' as possible by moving the cubes. This enables children to see what we mean by 'averaging things out'. Depending upon the data collected, it may not always be possible to create completely equal towers (see Figure 8.3) but we then have the opportunity to notice and discuss how we would describe our data when our average appears to fall between whole numbers.

(Continued)

(Continued)

Figure 8.3   Exploring 'mean' average using interlocking cubes

Assessment and review

Listening in and recording children's comments, observing their activity and careful questioning will enable ongoing feedback and inform whole-class reflection.

As children explore the concepts of equality, more/less, approximately equal and difference, it is important that they transfer this understanding to other contexts so that they see 'temperature' as an application of these generic skills. Ask children to build cube towers that represent people's ages, the height of buildings in metres, etc. so that they can notice and explain equality, inequality and difference, and realize that their skills are highly transferable.

Understanding 'units' of measure

In common with the 'newspaper' task, this activity brings about discussion and application of exist-ing number relationships with regard to the unit of measure being used on a thermometer. Again, it is easy to assume children have made sense of this concept because they can talk in terms of 'degrees' but careful questioning often reveals misconceptions born out of limited life experience. The experience of feeling and talking about temperature, using thermometers daily and using these skills in science activities, etc. cannot be stressed enough. For example:

- What does the symbol ° mean?
- What 'unit of measure' are we using?
- How many units of measure can we see on the thermometer? Carry out research into their differences and why there is more than one unit. Explore the historical use of 'Celsius' and 'Centigrade'.

Create a conversion graph to help children work with the different units of measure on a thermom-eter. Is there any other information you could include to make the comparative measures more meaningful? For example, the temperature of boiling water, when water freezes, a very hot day in the UK?

The above could then be used to generate questions to be investigated in science: for example, the rate at which water cools in different conditions, or comparing temperatures in different locations around school at the same time of day:

- What other 'units of measure' do we know about?
- Can we use tenths and hundredth of degrees as we do with other measures?

Extension and variation

Use national newspapers (current or older) to compare temperatures around the UK and plot these on a UK map.

Compare historic weather data from different areas of the UK that are known to the children using met office archives.

Again, build towers with interlocking cubes to represent the temperatures, using two colours of cubes in sticks of ten to encourage children to use place value rather than count in ones – an essential transition in becoming an efficient calculator. Transfer the concrete model to a vertical number line to calculate differences and label.

Use data to create questions, for example:

- The maximum temperature in Glasgow on Monday was 6°C and the minimum was –4°C. What is the difference in these temperatures and therefore the 'range'?
- Explore the language used to describe temperatures below freezing. Colloquially, people would say 'minus four' but in mathematics we would read this as 'negative four'. It is important to understanding that –4°C relates to four degrees below zero degrees Celsius or freezing point.
- At midday, the temperature was 4 degrees higher in London on Wednesday than on Tuesday. On Wednesday it was 19°C, what temperature was it at midday on Tuesday?
- Use the met office website to search for information on your local area over time. Notice patterns and describe changes. How would a day like this feel? What might you wear? How do you know?
- Compare temperatures at different times of the year in your local area. What might be expected and why?
- Contrast different times of the year in two locations in the UK. What differences would be expected due to the position of places in the UK, distance from the sea, near mountains, whether west, east, etc?
- Contrast two locations, one in the UK and one internationally (perhaps on the equator) at different times of the year. Does everywhere in the world have seasons?

Get children to explore which graphs best show temperature variation over time and which best show contrasting temperatures. Compare this with information given on travel websites and in holiday brochures.

Further cross-curricular links

The met office holds a vast amount of historical data regarding temperatures across the UK. This offers a wealth of opportunities for making comparisons over time as well as for beginning to spot and predict meteorological patterns and trends.

(Continued)

(Continued)

Look out for spreadsheets comparing data over different periods of time as well as satellite images of the UK that clearly show mountain ranges, urban and rural areas, rivers, etc. The photographs of the UK under snow are particularly stunning.

Such investigations lend themselves to high-quality work with statistics and offer all children the opportunity to work with real and meaningful data that can easily be accessed at home as well as in school.

CONCLUSION

In this chapter we have looked at how accessible and meaningful a simple starting point, such as a newspaper, can be as a way of enhancing mathematical thinking, and allowing children to notice and appreciate the many forms and uses of numbers across the curriculum. By beginning with numbers in context, we are far more likely to ignite children's interest and curiosity resulting in far higher levels of engagement and resilience. This in turn leads to an increased willingness to explore, question, construct and connect ideas that are essential for applying mathematics skilfully in everyday life.

FURTHER READING

Anghileri, J (2008) *Developing Number Sense: Progression in the Middle Years*. London: Continuum.

Ball, J (2005) *Think of a Number*. London: Dorling Kindersley.

Ball, J (2016) *Mathmagicians*. London: Dorling Kindersley.

Boaler, J (2008) *The Elephant in the Classroom: Helping Children Learn and Love Maths*. London: Souvenir Press.

Coats, L (2000) *Nigel's Numberless World*. London: Dorling Kindersley.

Fosnot, CT and **Dolk, M** (2011) *Young Mathematicians at Work – Constructing Number Sense, Addition, and Subtraction*. New York: Heinemann.

Gattengo, C (1988) *Teaching to inspire, not to inform*, ATM conference. Available at: www.atm.org.uk/Caleb-Gattegno.

Haylock, D (2014) *Mathematics Explained for Primary Teachers*. 5th edn. London: Sage.

Haylock, D and **Cockburn, A** (2013) *Understanding Mathematics for Young Children*. 4th edn. London: Sage.

Phillips, R (2000) *Numbers: Facts, Figures and Fiction*. Cambridge: Cambridge University Press.

9
LANGUAGES AND MATHEMATICS

PAULINE PALMER AND SARAH LISTER

IN THIS CHAPTER

This chapter:

- shows you how languages and mathematics can be taught together
- includes key French vocabulary for mathematics teaching
- includes tasks for exploring shapes and the vocabulary you need to do this
- explores synergies in the learning and teaching of mathematics and languages.

There are significant similarities between teaching modern foreign languages and mathematics. Both subjects can provoke anxiety and result in negative attitudes, a lack of confidence and an unwillingness to 'have a go' for fear of being wrong. Our aim is to encourage learners to engage in collaborative activities that are fun and where it does not matter if mistakes are made, as everyone is learning together.

Mathematics is a language, in itself. It has its own specific vocabulary, including words such as 'tessellating hexagons'. It 'borrows' from everyday language but uses words in very specific ways, such as 'face', 'tables' and 'take-away' and this can cause a lot of confusion among young learners. Mathematics has its own 'grammar', for example, the convention for rounding numbers and uses a great deal of supporting language that learners, especially those with English as an additional language, can find particularly tricky. Solving problems and developing reasoning, key aims of the current national curriculum, require that learners communicate their ideas clearly and allow them to experience mathematics as meaningful.

However, there are useful synergies between approaches to pedagogy in the two subject areas. Both benefit from the use of visual prompts and practical tasks. Moreover, repetition and use of key vocabulary in a meaningful context is central to the ability to communicate and demonstrate understanding.

The activities in this chapter are designed to teach and to reinforce key mathematical concepts, using the medium of French (though other languages could easily be substituted) and have been trialled by groups of practitioners and their classes.

PEDAGOGICAL APPROACH

This pedagogical approach is known as Content and Language Integrated Learning (CLIL). Marsh (2002: 15) defines CLIL as 'any dual-focused educational context in which an additional language, thus not usually the first language of the learners involved, is used as a medium in the teaching and learning of non-language content'.

This approach is used widely across parts of Europe and beyond. Research indicates that combining the subjects in this way does not hold learners back in either area. Placing the emphasis on content rather than language has the potential to be mutually beneficial for both the content subject and the language. Marsh (2002) argues that the dual purpose and focus of CLIL pedagogy provides a more cognitively challenging and authentic platform for language acquisition and use, while providing meaningful and new contexts for learners to revisit key mathematical concepts. Engaging with content language can enable learners to access ideas in a new way, allowing for some repetition of the key elements, to reinforce these ideas.

However, this approach does more than this. Adopting a CLIL approach can deepen children's thinking as they search for and make connections between mathematics and language. Thus, there are considerable cognitive benefits. As teachers, we want learners to learn how to solve problems and to learn through solving problems. It could be argued that CLIL provides the context and the opportunity to demonstrate understanding. According to Maljers et al. (2010), CLIL is a dual-focused approach where the subject content is delivered using an additional language, used for the teaching of content and language simultaneously. The objective of CLIL is to promote both content and language learning.

Whether you are a linguist, a mathematics specialist, or a general class teacher, looking to develop your practice and find new ideas, we urge you to give this approach a go. Please note that some of these activities may also be suitable for younger children, depending on when your school introduces modern foreign languages.

2D SHAPES IN ART

These activities enable children to explore a range of 2D shapes within a real-life context. As they explore, they are recognizing non-prototypical shapes in different orientations. Using the target language to discuss the various properties and positions can enhance their own understanding of the key concepts.

ACTIVITY

Make a shape picture

Make a collage after the style of Picasso or another artist.

Resources

- sets of plastic 2D shapes
- large [A3] prints of Picasso [or other] art work, sufficient for small groups to have one each.
- scissors
- glue
- paper for shapes and background.

National curriculum and mathematical understanding links

Suitable for: age 7–8.

Mathematical understanding: to compare and classify geometric shapes, including quadrilaterals and triangles, based on their properties and sizes.

Modern Foreign Languages (MFL): speaking, listening, reading and writing.

Setting the scene

Show the children the chosen piece of work, possibly giving some preliminary facts about the artist and the painting. The children are encouraged to talk to a partner about what they can see in the picture. Introduce the appropriate French vocabulary and sentence structure required to talk about the shapes in the picture.

Trigger questions

English	French
What shapes can you see?	Tu peux voir quelles formes?
How many sides are there in this shape?	Il y a combien de côtés dans cette forme?
How many corners are there in this shape?	Il y a combien de coins dans cette forme?
How many right angles are there in this shape?	Il y a combien d'angles droits dans cette forme?
How many acute angles are there in this shape?	Il y a combien d'angles aigus dans cette forme?
How many obtuse angles are there in this shape?	Il y combien d'angles obtus dans cette forme?
How many are there of this shape? [insert shape name as appropriate]	Il y a combien de (triangles)?
Are all these shapes of the same size?	Est-ce que toutes les formes sont du même taille?
Are they in the same position?	Est-ce que tous (les triangles) dans la même position?

(Continued)

(Continued)

On each table provide a laminated A3 version of the questions and a box of 2D shapes. A prompt sheet (see Figure 9.1) could also be provided.

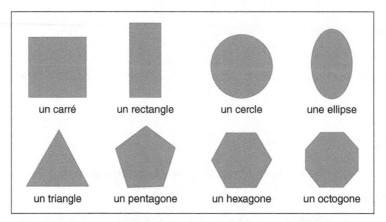

Figure 9.1   Les Formes Géométriques 2D prompt sheet

Children now search the paintings on their tables to try and find as many shapes as they can, with reference to the prompt sheet and/or the sets of 2D shapes provided. Each table must report back on what they have found to another table, using the French sentences provided, substituting the correct shape name and properties.

Having explored the shapes in the painting, the children work individually to create their own shape picture, after the style of Picasso, using either pre-cut shapes or their own versions. The teacher could set the criteria: for example, all triangles or the children could simply create their own picture.

Review and reflect

Children display their work/share with another table and explain, in French, what shapes they have used.

Ask the children to describe their work to each other and to ask questions of each other, in the second language: for example, 'How many acute angled triangles have you used?'

Assessment

Assess as above for the language element and with reference to the set criteria. For example, have the children only used triangles to create their picture? In terms of the art, children could be encouraged to peer assess the completed picture, for example, using three stars and a wish.

Follow-up tasks

The art work could be displayed with accompanying questions or captions written in French.

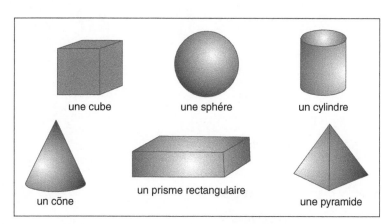

Figure 9.2   Les Formes Géométriques 3D prompt sheet

Children examine other works of art, including sculpture and lead into 3D shape work – for example the work of Matisse or Mondrian.

KEY VOCABULARY FOR 2D SHAPES

LES COULEURS

bleu	blue
orange	orange
gris	grey
vert	green
rose	pink
violet	purple
rouge	red
noir	black
marron/brun	brown
blanc	white
jaune	yellow

LES FORMES

un triangle	a triangle
un rectangle	a rectangle

un cercle	a circle
un carré	a square
un hexagone	a hexagon
un pentagone	a pentagon
un octagone	an octagon
une ovale	an oval
un losange	a rhombus
un cerf volant	a kite
un parallélogramme	a parallelogram
un trapeze	a trapezium
un triangle isocele	an isosceles triangle
un triangle équilatéral	an equilateral triangle
un triangle a un angle droit/ avec un angle droit:	a right-angled triangle
un triangle avec un angle obtus	an obtuse angle triangle
assembler en mosaique	create a shape picture

LES CHIFFRES

un	one
deux	two
trois	three
quatre	four
cinq	five
six	six
sept	seven
huit	eight
neuf	nine
dix	ten
C'est quelle forme?	What shape is it?
C'est un/une ...	It's ...
Il y a combien de côtés?	How many sides are there?

Il y a ... côtés	There are ... sides
Un triangle a combien de côtés?	A triangle has how many sides?
Vous pouvez voir combien de triangles?	How many triangles can you see?
Je peux voir... triangles.	I can see ... triangles
Il y a combien de triangles différents?	How many different triangles are there?
Il y a ...	There are ... different triangles
Qu'est-ce que vous pouvez voir?	What can you see?
Je peux voir...	I can see
Par exemple: je peux voir les rectangles.	For example: I can see rectangles.

EXPLORING ANGLES

ACTIVITY

Angle eaters

This activity focuses on children being able to recognize right angles within objects, using simple home-made equipment, and to find out how many right, acute or obtuse angles there are in the classroom.

Resources

Angle eaters are made with lollipop sticks connected together using split pins (Figure 9.3).

Figure 9.3   Angle eaters

(Continued)

(Continued)

You may also find the following items useful:

- a selection of prepared shapes that have a variety of different angles
- other objects or images
- angle measurers (protractors)
- vocabulary prompt sheet in French
- recording sheets, in French - see template.

National curriculum and mathematical understanding links

Suitable for: age 7-9.

Mathematical understanding: to recognize angles as a measure of turn; to identify right angles; to identify acute and obtuse angle and compare angles by size.

Modern Foreign Languages (MFL): speaking, listening, reading and writing.

Setting the scene

Create a scenario in which it is important to know about all the angles in the room.

There could be a new rule that has just been made by the government about classroom layout and equipment. The children need to help you collect information that will show whether or not the classroom complies with this rule.

Alternatively, it could be that a strange new creature has been reported in your area: an angle-eating beetle. If this creature gets access to materials and resources in the classroom, it may destroy them, so we have to find out which ones need special protection.

Model how to make an 'angle eater' using two lollipop sticks (you may wish to predrill the holes, which need to be half way along the length of each stick). The sticks are attached together with a split pin.

As you complete each action, explain what you are doing in French.

Children repeat each phrase.

Children then work in pairs, one to give the instructions, one to make the angle eater. They use these to make right angles and/or angles greater than or less than a right angle, turning the 'arms' of the sticks to do this.

The children may also decorate the sticks by attaching sets of thin card teeth, to create a 'mouth'.

Now set the task, in French, to find out how many right/acute/obtuse angles an object has, again modelling this first, using French.

The children then explore the angles in a range of shapes, objects and features found within the classroom and decide whether each angle is a right angle or greater than a right angle, introducing the terminology of obtuse/acute/reflex angle.

They could explore the effect of opening the blades on scissors, turning over a large number of pages in an opened book, opening and closing doors, using switches, for example.

Trigger questions (to be asked in French)

English	French
Is this a right angle?	Est-ce que c'est un angle droit?
How many right angles can you find in the classroom?	Tu peux trouver combien d'angles droits dans la salle de classe?
Is this less than a right angle (acute angle)?	Est-ce que c'est moins qu'un angle droit/un angle aigu?
Is this more than a right angle (obtuse angle)?	Est-ce que c'est plus qu'un angle droit/un angle obtus?

Exploration

Children work in pairs to explore a selection of objects and shapes within their classroom, deciding how many right angles each one has. They need to use the appropriate French phrases. They could take it in turns to count the right angles, using their angle eater and to complete the sheet, in French to say, for example: 'this is a ..., it has ... right angles' (number to be written in words).

Review and reflect

Check that the children are using the angle eaters correctly and, if used, are completing the recording sheets.

Assessment

Invite children to report back in French, demonstrating the objects, shapes and features that they have looked at, and saying how many right/acute/obtuse angles each one has. Their peers can assess the accuracy of the mathematics and French.

Follow-up tasks

Children could explore other areas of the school, including the outside areas. They could create an angle trail for others to follow.

Children could create stories about the 'angle eater' beetles.

The angle eaters could be laid out on a flat horizontal surface to create 2D shapes. Children could explore the effects of 'opening and closing' the angle eaters in order to change the enclosed shapes and interior angles. They could also discuss exterior angles, which may involve the use of the term 'reflex angles'.

KEY VOCABULARY FOR ANGLES

Tournez ...	Turn ...
Trouvez ...	Find ...
un angle droit	a right angle
un angle plus grand que ...	an angle bigger than ...
un angle moins (de/que)	an angle less than
Tu dois trouver ...	You must find ...
Il faut trouver ...	You must find ...
aigu	acute
obtus	obtuse
à gauche	to the left
à droite	to the right
Tu dois tourner à travers quel angle?	Through what angle do you need to turn?
or	
Il faut tourner a travers quel angle?	Through what angle do you need to turn?
C'est un angle ...	It's a ... angle
Je sais	I know
parce que	because

TREASURE HUNT

This activity focuses on developing an understanding of positional movement and the fact that co-ordinates may be used to identify locations on a grid.

These tasks enable children to utilize positional vocabulary, in the target language, in a meaningful context.

ACTIVITY

Treasure hunt

Hide some 'treasure' at a given grid point on a large-scale grid laid out on the floor. Children have to locate the treasure by interpreting information given to them.

Once you have modelled this, let the children work in small groups, each one working on an individual grid, and each child taking it in turns to 'hide' the treasure.

Having had this practical experience, children can create their own treasure maps on squared paper. Make a copy of each one so that children can play, in pairs, to locate the treasure.

Resources

Ideally, use the hall or similar large space to do this activity.

You will need the following materials and equipment:

- several large grids, at least five-by-five, laid out on the floor, with *x* and *y* axes labelled; and appropriate numbers/letters on a card
- mini-whiteboards and pens
- you may also wish to use squared paper for the extension activities.

National curriculum and mathematical understanding links

Suitable for: age 7-9.

Mathematical understanding: using geometry; to describe positions on a 2D grid as co-ordinates in the first quadrant.

Modern Foreign Languages (MFL): speaking, listening, reading and writing.

Setting the scene

Set the scene explaining that there is some treasure buried within the grid. Keep a written record of the location, to reveal when the children have found the correct location on the grid. Children suggest a possible grid point and one child must stand on it. Then say how many points away they are, in French, with reference to the horizontal and vertical: for example, 'You are three points out' (note that you do not say in which direction). Record the number of points out, on a mini-whiteboard for the child to hold, as a point of reference. Children predict which grid point they now think has the hidden treasure. Again, a child goes and stands on this point, and again, you say how far away the child is. This is recorded on a mini-whiteboard. Continue until the treasure is found.

Following on from the whole-class demonstration, children work in small groups on their own five-by-five grids. One child decides where the treasure is going to be hidden and records this for reference, keeping it out of sight of the rest of the group. The rest of the group work as before.

Trigger questions

Ask the children to consider what options there might be for the location of the treasure, given what they already know. Their reply could be, for example: 'two up and one along to the left'.

(Continued)

(Continued)

English	French
Where could the treasure be?	Ou se trouve le tresor?
You are three [points] out.	Vous vous trompez par trois.
Move two squares up and one along to the left.	Montez deux carrés et un carré a gauche.
You have found the treasure.	Vous avez trouvé le tresor.

Review and reflect

The teacher can go back to the first point and ask the children to suggest what the alternatives might be, for three points out. Have they found all the possibilities?

Assessment

Children can peer assess the accuracy of information given by the child who has 'hidden the treasure'.

Follow-up tasks

This activity could also be played like a 'Battleship' game, using squared paper with a barrier between each pair of children. Child A is responsible for identifying the grid point. Child B has to try and predict where this might be, offering a named grid point. Child A then has to say how many moves out they are.

OTHER ACTIVITIES TO EXPLORE POSITION AND MOVEMENT

DANCE

You will need some suitable music for this activity, preferably from the country of the language you are teaching, for example, France.

Music is played and then halted briefly. Give children instructions in French, starting with simple instructions that build up in complexity: to move forward/ backwards; move to the left or the right; to take a specified number of steps; take small/large steps; moving slowly or quickly (single instructions, building up in complexity) with the music, for example: 'Take five small steps to the left'.

MAZES

Get children to work in pairs on a maze activity. Child A gives child B instructions to move around a series of objects that have been placed on the floor to create a maze. 'Bee-bots' or similar programmable toys can also be used. Children could also record their ideas on squared paper.

English	French
Take one step forward.	Prenez un pas en avance.
Take two steps backward.	Prenez deux pas en arrière.
Turn to the left.	Tournez à gauche.
Turn to the right.	Tournez à droite.
Take two small steps.	Prenez deux petits pas.
Take three big steps.	Prenez trois grands pas.
Take four slow steps.	Prenez quatre pas lentement.
Take five quick steps.	Prenez cinq pas rapidement.
Turn clockwise.	Tournez dans le sens horaire.
Turn anti-clockwise.	Tournez dans le sens anti-horaire.

KEY VOCABULARY FOR POSITION AND MOVEMENT

Avancez ...	Go forward ...
Recoulez ...	Go back ...
Prenez ...	Take ...
un/deux pas en avance	one/two steps forward
un/deux pas en arrière	one/two steps back
un/deux pas a gauche	one/two steps to the left
un/deux pas a droite	one/two steps to the right
Prenez un/deux grand pas	Take one/two big steps ...
Prenez un/deux petits pas	Take one/two small steps ...
à droite	to the right
à gauche	to the left
dans le sens horaire	clockwise
sens anti-horaire	anti-clockwise
Tournez ...	Turn ...
Allez tout droit ...	Go straight on ...

Allez en arrière ...	Go backwards ...
lentement	slowly
rapidement	quickly
Trouvez ...	Find ...
le trésor	the treasure
C'est situé ...	It's located ...
un carré	a square
Vous vous trompez par...	You are out by ...
or	
Vous êtes hors par...	You are out by ...
par exemple	for example

CONCLUSION

We hope that you enjoy working on these activities with your class and they inspire you to make regular links between mathematics and language learning. All teachers are teachers of language – the CLIL approach enables new language and content to be taught together in a meaningful way.

REFERENCES

Maljers, A, Marsh, D, Wolff, D, Genesee, F, Frigols-Martín, M and **Mehisto, P** (2010) based on D Marsh, and D Wolff, (eds), (2007) *Windows on CLIL: Content and Language Integrated Learning in the European Spotlight*. The Hague: European Platform for Dutch Education, and Graz: European Centre for Modern Languages.

Marsh, D (2002) *Using Languages to Learn and Learning to Use Languages*. TIE_CLIL Professional Development Course, TIE-CLIL: Milan.

10
ART AND MATHEMATICS

DIANA COBDEN

--- IN THIS CHAPTER ---

This chapter:

- explores how the two subjects of art and mathematics complement each other
- presents activities for valuable learning in both subjects
- shows how art can develop children's creativity and self esteem
- considers the value of perspective and abstract art for the learning and teaching of mathematics.

From the earliest times in human history, evidence has been found of art in some form. Even in the New Stone Age there is much evidence that people were making and colouring pottery, decorated with simple repeating geometric patterns. They also wove cloth on simple looms and made baskets. Over the centuries, these skills have been developed enabling artists, designers, potters, sculptors, musicians and architects to produce increasingly sophisticated work. What do art and mathematics have in common? In fact, both are very much about geometry, design and pattern, both numerical and geometrical.

By linking mathematics and art, children can appreciate that the two subjects complement each other, so that mathematics can inform artistic developments, and art can be derived from mathematical patterns, form and ratio. The two subjects can both help to develop the skills of creativity, self-expression, pattern spotting and representation. Linking them together can provide particularly valuable learning experiences for all children, in particular those children who may be more interested in art.

It is thought that the ancient Egyptians might have been the first people to use geometric patterns from as early as 4000–3500 BCE, although Neolithic pottery has been found in Hungary, decorated with what appear to be triangular number patterns.

When thinking about art in Roman times, people are most likely to talk about mosaic floor and wall decorations. Although these often included stylized pictures of their Gods and animals, they all included interesting uses of geometric patterns that can be investigated in the classroom. The people who laid the mosaics may have shown 'pattern books' for their clients to choose from. Islamic art also developed geometric designs to decorate their buildings. Sometimes the designs consisted of only one or two shapes but different designs and patterns might have been used on the shapes.

The most striking examples of architecture to have been found from ancient times, and probably the most recognizable of the earliest forms of architecture, are the pyramids and the best known of these structures are those built in Egypt about 4500 years ago. The most famous of the Egyptian pyramids, the Great Pyramid of Giza, was the tallest building in the world until the Eiffel Tower was built in 1889.

The earliest pyramid structures, called ziggurats, were built in Mesopotamia from sun-dried mud bricks. They had a square base but unlike the more familiar Egyptian pyramids, the sides were stepped, rather than smooth. The Mayans, and others, built similar types of pyramids in South America but these tended to have a temple-like structure on the top, whereas the Egyptian pyramids were built as tombs to the Pharaohs.

During the Renaissance, artists wanted to paint in a more realistic way. The German artist, Albrecht Dürer (1471-1525) is thought to be the first artist to introduce perspective into his work. This led to art being much more representational of the real world and it also revived a Greek doctrine that depicting art is a mathematical law, in that the three-dimensional world is being recreated on the canvas in two dimensions. Look at one of Dürer's later paintings, such as the Adoration of the Magi and see how the use of perspective can focus the viewer's attention on the foreground, while the people and scene in the background appear to be further away and smaller. In addition to his painting, Dürer published three books on geometry and others on human proportions.

The use of perspective can be demonstrated in the classroom by showing large 3D shapes, such as a cardboard box: discuss the shape of each face, ask what shapes can be seen when it is viewed from different angles – is it possible that none of the faces look like rectangles? Talk about the changes in the angles and the apparent size of the box when it is nearer and further away. Make a display by hanging both 3D and 2D shapes in the classroom so they can swing freely and children can talk about what they see. It is also interesting to hang 3D skeletal solids where they can cast reflections that can be recorded in 2D and used to create new and interesting designs.

Tessellations have been used in art since very early times. The Romans used small 'tesserae' to create mosaics and Islamic artists used polygonal tiles to create tiling patterns. In the twentieth century, artists began to develop new ways of using tessellations to create works of art; most notable of these artists was M.C. Escher. Escher took the shapes to a completely new level of creativity by changing shapes into fantastic tessellating creatures. In addition, Escher also created artworks based on other mathematical ideas, such as the Möbius Strip, notably Möbius Strip II, with its giant ants crawling around the strip.

In the twentieth century some artists started to work in a more abstract way and to express their ideas in line, colour and shape. The Cubism movement led by Pablo Picasso and Georges Braque, used multiple perspectives and inspired many artists to work in the abstract, such as Piet Mondrian, Victor Vasarely and Ben Nicholson. Their works consisted of arrangements of geometric shapes to create patterns of form, colour and line. Their ideas were based on the view of Plato that the 'highest form of beauty lies not in the forms of the real world but in geometry'.

The activities in this chapter focus on:

- Roman and Islamic art
- pyramids
- changing shapes.

ACTIVITY

Roman and Islamic art

Although the Romans built some of the most magnificent temples and churches and their artists created some wonderful sculptures, which were very much influenced by the Greeks, they are possibly best known for their mosaics. These were used to decorate the walls and floors of important buildings. Many of the floors, in particular, have survived in a well-preserved state and can still be seen in this country and around Europe and the Mediterranean. These designs were made using small squares usually arranged in geometric designs.

Often mosaic designers would show their clients the different designs they had created, so children's designs could be used to make a class book of Roman mosaic designs.

Resources

- 2cm-squared paper or card
- colouring pencils or pens
- black and white squares of card
- triangle grid paper
- pairs of compasses, angle measurers and rulers
- paper circles.

Useful links

NRICH printable online resources: http://nrich.maths.org/8506)

National curriculum and mathematical understanding links

Suitable for: age 7 and above.

Objectives: to learn about symmetry, shape and angles through practical activities linked to Roman mosaics and Islamic art; to develop an understanding of symmetry and the effects of translating, reflecting or rotating designs; to find fractions in design work; to calculate angles and use the calculations to draw shapes and to determine whether or not shapes will tessellate.

Exploring Roman mosaic patterns

Display some pictures of Roman mosaics, for example, some of the square designs from Silchester. Study some examples of tiling patterns from Roman floors; focus particularly on the borders, as these are more

(Continued)

(Continued)

likely to show repeating patterns, that have been translated, rotated, or reflected. Discuss how the patterns are created before giving children the opportunity to design their own mosaic borders.

For younger children, a starting point can be to create different four-by-four square patterns, using black and white squares. Rules can be set about the numbers of each colour to use, for example, half black and half white. The ideas can be shared to find how many different patterns have been found. Choose one and demonstrate how the design can be translated, reflected or rotated to create border patterns.

Extend the activity by cutting some of the black and white squares in half initially and then in quarters diagonally, for children to investigate different arrangements to create a tile. One of the designs can be selected to create a symmetrical border pattern. Encourage discussion about new shapes that are created when the initial design is joined symmetrically in some way.

Older children can create designs on one quarter of a piece of four-by-four squared paper and reflect the design into the other three quarters.

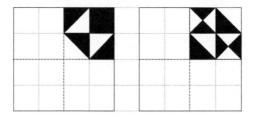

Figure 10.1   Reflect a tile design

A number of square tiles divided in half diagonally and coloured black and white will be needed. Children, in groups, can explore the number of different ways of putting four of the tiles in a straight line. Once they have explored as many as possible, they can discuss the symmetry of each one. Ask children to choose one of the designs and make a 16-by-16 design on squared paper. Compare the designs and discuss the transformations that were used.

Set a challenge to find as many possible tile designs that can be drawn inside a three-by-three square using four straight lines to join the two dots on each edge of the square. Set the rule that only four lines can be used and each dot can only be used once. This investigation can be extended using a four-by-four square, three dots along each side and six lines.

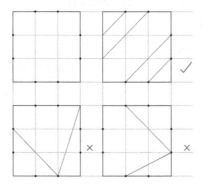

Figure 10.2   Create a tile design

Islamic art

The designs used in Islamic art are very symbolic and works of art are made to the glory of God. The representation of people is considered to be blasphemous and so geometric shapes are used, with the circle representing either the universe or heaven. The square is thought of as the world with the four corners being the points of the compass and the triangle is the smallest possible 2D shape; both of these shapes, and the hexagon, can be drawn within the circle, using a pair of compasses and a ruler. A pair of compasses is considered to be a sacred tool, with the stationary point being the centre of the Universe and the moving arm representing the rotations of the planets in the heavens.

Exploring stars

Many of the designs used in Islamic art are based on star shapes using a circle as the starting point to draw hexagons and octagons. Tessellations of these shapes can be first explored using pattern blocks, or a similar resource, and drawn on squared or hexagonal paper.

Show how the circle can be used for drawing different polygons and stars by asking, first three children, then four, etc. to stand in a circle and either throw a ball to each other or pass a ball of string from one to another and say the name of the shape. Change the moves so the ball is passed to every other person in a clockwise direction, discussing what to do when there are six people. Make a generalization about the stars with odd and even numbers.

Younger children can record the moves and star shapes on paper with pre-printed circles with different numbers of equally spaced dots on the circumference (see NRICH in 'Useful links' above). What happens if the moves around the circle go to every third dot in a clockwise direction?

Challenge children to make eight-pointed stars by folding paper circles into eighths, marking eight points on the circumference of the circle, then drawing an eight-pointed star. Can six-pointed stars be made using the same technique? Discuss what they know about calculating the sizes of the angles around the centre, that is, 360° divided by eight or by six? Can they calculate the interior angles of the triangles at each point and the interior angles of the octagon?

Another method for drawing the circles and the hexagon requires the use of a pair of compasses.

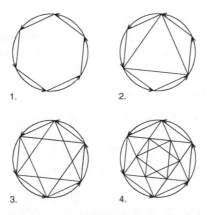

Figure 10.3   Drawing hexagons and stars

(Continued)

(Continued)

- Use a pair of compasses to draw a circle and, keeping them open at the same measurement as the radius, mark six points around the edge of the circle and join them to form a hexagon. Why does this work?

- Join up every second point to create an equilateral triangle.

- Join the other three points to make another triangle to form a six-pointed star with the triangle pointing upwards thought to be pointing to heaven and the other to the earth.

- Join the points of the interior hexagon in the same way as for the first to form another star.

- Continue to draw more stars.

Give time for children to look for patterns in the arrangement of the stars and to make generalizations about the number patterns.

Review and reflect

In groups, discuss the ways a circle could be divided into equal parts before drawing the six- and eight-pointed stars. Then discuss how they could measure the angle between each radius at the centre of the circle. What would the angles be if they wanted to draw stars with different numbers of points, for example, 10, 12, 20?

Assessment

Ask children to explain what they have learned about symmetry and how a pattern or design might be changed if it is reflected, rotated or translated.

Can they explain how to calculate the measurements of angles where three or more shapes meet at one point?

Follow-up tasks

- Find ways to create repeating geometric patterns using octagons or hexagons with another shape.

- Make star designs using folded paper shapes.

- Draw a Rangoli pattern on squared 'dotty' paper. Rangoli patterns are used by Sikhs and Hindus to decorate their temples and homes during the festival of Diwali. Name the new shapes that are formed as the design is completed.

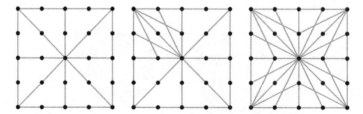

Figure 10.4   Creating a Rangoli pattern using reflection

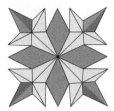

Figure 10.5   A completed Rangoli pattern

ACTIVITY

Pyramids and number patterns

Resources

- interlocking cubes
- linking triangles, such as Polydron or Clixi
- 1cm or 2cm square grid paper
- 2cm triangle grid paper
- 2cm hexagonal grid paper.

National curriculum and mathematical understanding links

Suitable for: age 8 and above.

Objectives: to explore number patterns that result from constructing increasing sizes and types of pyramid and begin to predict how the patterns will continue.

Setting the scene

The earliest pyramid structures called ziggurats were built from sun-dried mud bricks and unlike the Egyptian pyramids, the sides were stepped rather than straight, and built up from a square base. The Mayans, and others, built similar types of pyramid in South American but these tended to have a temple-like structure on the top.

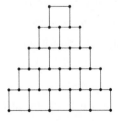

Figure 10.6   Cross-section of a pyramid made using consecutive square numbers for each layer

(Continued)

(Continued)

Build a ziggurat

Use cubes to build a ziggurat, starting with one cube, to form the top.

Ask children questions about the structures:

- What do you notice about the number of bricks needed for each layer?
- Can you find a way to work out the number of bricks needed for a ziggurat with any number of steps?
- Can you make a ziggurat with larger steps? How does this change the number patterns?
- Can a stepped pyramid be made using any other shape? If so, what number patterns can you find?

This activity enables children to explore patterns within consecutive and alternate square numbers and to recognize how they can be used in real situations.

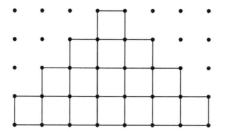

Figure 10.7   Cross-section of pyramid built from alternate square numbers

Square-based pyramids

The famous Egyptian pyramids had square bases, like the ziggurat, but the sides were triangular. Imagine that each face of the pyramid was built with small triangles.

Use interlocking triangles and squares to make the smallest possible square-based pyramid:

Discuss how many of each shape were used and what would be needed to make the pyramid larger. Ask what would happen in the following scenarios:

- The pyramid is twice the size. How many triangles were used?
- How many triangles have their base at the bottom of each row?
- How many triangles have their base at the top of each row?
- What if a pyramid is three times larger than the first one? Or four times larger? Or any times larger?
- What happens if a triangle-based pyramid is made?
- What other pyramids could you make with a different-shaped base and the sides made using triangles?
- Explore the number patterns on one face of a pyramid, for example, the number of triangles added on each row, and the number of triangles altogether as the face grows, etc.

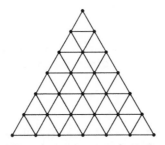

Figure 10.8   A triangular face made from smaller triangles

Modern pyramids

Outside the Louvre in Paris, is a very modern glass pyramid. Designed by the architect, I.M. Pei, it was built in the 1980s and forms the entrance to the main museum. The height of the pyramid is 22m and each edge at the base measures approximately 35m. Around the outside are three smaller pyramids with reflecting pools and fountains.

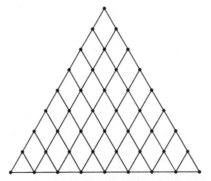

Figure 10.9   Diagram of the triangular face of the Louvre Pyramid showing the shapes used in its construction

Display a range of pictures of the Louvre Pyramid and ask children, working in groups, to write as many mathematical facts as possible about the structure. These might include:

- the shapes used
- numbers of each shape on one face, and on all the faces
- number patterns.

The height of the pyramid is 21m and the base of each face is just over 35m. The pyramid was constructed from 625 rhombuses and 118 triangles and the floor area is 1000 sq. metres. Part of the original building is incorporated into the fourth side of the structure, which makes it difficult for children to calculate the number of each shape needed. A scale drawing might be helpful.

(Continued)

(Continued)

Children could work with a hypothetical situation to make the calculations a little more accessible, for example, floor area is 900 sq. metres and the sides of each rhombus are 3m.

Tetrahedral numbers

A display outside the Royal Armouries Museum in Portsmouth features cannon balls arranged in tetrahedral shapes. Investigate the numbers of cannon balls that would be needed for different sizes of display. Models can be made using Plasticine or Playdough shaped into spheres of the same size.

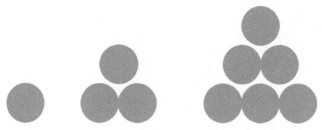

Figure 10.10   The first three layers of a tetrahedron made using spheres of the same size

Growing tetrahedra

Make several of the smallest possible tetrahedra using interlocking equilateral triangles. Investigate the number needed to make the next size, so that each face shows four triangles.

Is it possible to fill the whole space with small tetrahedra? Or is another shape or shapes needed?

What about the next size of tetrahedron? And the next?

What number patterns can be found?

Trigger questions

- What pattern of numbers do you find if each face is made using hexagons?
- If hexagons were used on each face, would you need to use any other shape as well?
- Can you work out a way to find the number of shapes you need for any size of pyramid?
- Can you explain how you found the total numbers of each shape for your pyramids?

Review and reflect

Can you find any other shapes that could be used to create pyramids? Do you think you could use triangles that are not regular, such as scalene triangles? How many different shapes could be used for the pyramid bases if the sides are triangular? Could any other shapes be used to make ziggurats?

Assessment

It is useful to ask open-ended questions so that children have to explain their reasoning. Can they explain why the number patterns grow as they do; how they worked out the numbers for any size of pyramid, etc? It is also useful to ask if there was anything they did not understand.

Follow-up tasks

- How many different nets could you find for making a tetrahedron, or a square-based pyramid?

- Extend the number pattern tasks by exploring the number patterns in Pascal's Triangle. Ask children to identify the number patterns they found in constructing their pyramids, that is, square and triangle numbers. This could lead to children using modulo 2 or 3 and colouring identical numbers.

- Ask children to find out about the shapes and measurements of other large architectural London buildings, for example, the Gherkin, the Shard, the Cheese Grater and putting them in order of size. Designs for a structure using different shapes can be drawn from different viewpoints.

- The Egyptians developed a way of measuring the height of a pyramid. Can children find the method and use it to measure, for example, the height of the school, or a nearby tree?

- Find out how to create pyramids using origami.

ACTIVITY

Exploring new shapes

Resources

- card squares of the same size (blank) and A4 card marked into squares
- scissors
- 2cm-squared paper
- mirrors
- sticky tape
- paper strips.

National curriculum and mathematical understanding links

Suitable for: age 7 and above.

Objectives: to recognize the difference between regular and irregular polygons by reasoning about the side lengths and angles; to identify and name new polygons by counting the number of sides; to explain whether shapes will tessellate or not, by referring to the angles; to create artworks using mathematical ideas.

(Continued)

(Continued)

Setting the scene

Give children a selection of different regular polygons and ask them to demonstrate those that will tessellate on their own (equilateral triangle, square, regular hexagon) and to discuss why some regular polygons fit together without leaving gaps and others do not. Explain that they will be creating new shapes and investigating ways they can tessellate to make pictures and designs.

Three shapes into one

Give children two squares of the same size and ask them to cut one in half diagonally to make two isosceles right-angled triangles (IRATs). Ask them to investigate how many new shapes can be made using the three shapes. Edges of the same length must be placed alongside each other and must not overlap.

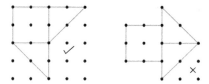

Figure 10.11   Correct and incorrect ways of joining the three shapes

By recording their new shapes on squared paper children will be able to discard any that are mirror images or rotations. It is possible to make seven new shapes (see Figure 10.12). Discuss what children notice about the new shapes. This might include:

- the number of sides
- angles
- names of new shapes
- symmetry properties.

Name all the new shapes and investigate which of them will tessellate on their own. Will they tessellate in more than one way?

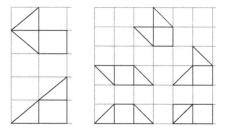

Figure 10.12   Seven possible shapes from a square and two IRATs

Explore tessellations using two or more of the shapes. Discuss why these shapes will or will not tessellate, in particular by referring to the angle measurements.

Suggest to children that they create a repeating pattern design using one of the tessellations to create a picture, a curtain fabric or carpet design.

Cut and move shapes

Study some of the works of M.C. Escher, who is probably the best-known artist to use tessellating designs to create pictures. Notice how he started with a shape and altered it to create amazing tessellations from novel shapes, many of which depict strange and interesting creatures. Study some of Escher's works and try to work how they were created.

Show children how to start simply with a square of card, cut a piece from one side and stick it on the opposite side to change the shape. Explain the pieces they cut off can be curved or straight and the important thing is to try to envisage what the final shape will be and how a number of the shapes will tessellate.

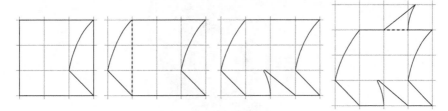

Figure 10.13   Transforming a square into a new tessellating shape (a fish?)

Once children have created a design they like, they can complete a picture showing the influence of Escher's work. Extend this activity by using different starting shapes, such as a rhombus or triangle. For each new shape, children can describe the movements they made when joining the cut-out pieces from the original shape to create the new shape.

The Möbius Strip

Show a copy of Escher's pictures of Möbius I and Möbius II. In pairs, children use a strip of paper to make a ring and count the faces. Show how to make a single twist to the strip before sticking it together and ask how many faces they can count now (see Figure 10.14). Allow thinking time before asking for suggestions. Drawing a line along the length of the loop will show that now it has only one face. Ask children to investigate:

- what happens if two twists are made? Or three twists?
- what are the outcomes if a cut is made along the middle of the band after one, two, or more twists are made instead of drawing a line?
- what generalizations can be made?

(Continued)

(Continued)

Figure 10.14   MC Escher's ants on a möbius strip

Trigger questions

- Can you explain how you worked to try and find all the different new shapes?

- Do you think that you could find more or fewer new shapes if you used four right-angled triangles? What makes you think that?

- What if you used four equilateral triangles? Or five?

- What if you make new shapes using different numbers of the same shape, for example, polyominoes (squares joined edge to edge) or polyiamonds (equilateral triangles joined edge to edge)?

Review and reflect

When you were trying to make new shapes from the square and two triangles, how did you make sure you had found all the possible new shapes? If you did this task again, would you do anything differently?

What shapes could be used as starting shapes for making a tessellating shape?

Assessment

When you were making three shapes into one how did you check that there were no shapes the same?

Can you explain why you needed to stick any pieces you cut from one side of the start shape to the opposite side?

Follow-up tasks

Make a Möbius Strip with a piece of card measuring 30 x 4cm. After it has been joined, design an insect that will look as though it is walking around the strip. Draw the insects 5cm long so they follow each other around the length of the Möbius Strip.

With the children study the work of Op Art movement, particularly that of Bridget Riley and Victor Vasarely. Create an artwork based on the way they used shape and colour to deceive the eye. Investigate curves of pursuit. Colour them in black and white, and then explore different ways to link curves.

Figure 10.15   An example of Op Art

FURTHER READING

ATM (2010) *Polygons, Dot-to-dot*. Derby: Association of Teachers of Mathematics.

Bezuszka, S, Kennedy, M and **Silvey, L** (1978) *Designs from Mathematical Patterns*. California: Creative Publications.

Escher Foundation (2000) *The Magic of M.C. Escher*. Thames and Hudson.

Field R (1998) *Geometric Patterns from Islamic Art and Architecture*, Diss: Tarquin Publications.

Field R (1996) *Geometric Patterns from Roman Mosaics*, Diss: Tarquin Publications.

Field R (1996) *Geometric Patterns from Tiles and Brickwork*, Diss: Tarquin Publications.

Field R (1996) *Geometric Patterns from Churches and Cathedrals*, Diss: Tarquin Publications.

Lam, TK and **Pope, S** (2016) *Learning Mathematics with Origami*. Derby: Association of Teachers of Mathematics.

Langdon, N and **Snape, C** (1984) *A Way with Maths*. Cambridge: Cambridge University Press.

Mottershead, L (1978) *Sources of Mathematical Discovery*. London: Blackwell. Available at: https://www.stem.org.uk/elibrary/resource/27178.

Seymour, D and **Britton, J** (1990) *Introduction to Tessellations*. New Jersey: Dale Seymour Publications.

Snape, C and **Scott, H** (1995) *Puzzles, Mazes and Numbers*. Cambridge: Cambridge University Press.

11

DRAMA AND MATHEMATICS

TONY COTTON AND HELEN TOFT

IN THIS CHAPTER

This chapter:

- considers the context of cross-curricular work in mathematics
- explores the possibilities of learning and teaching mathematics through drama
- highlights the importance of context to engage learners
- explains the 'Mantle of the expert' approach.

The ability to operate mathematically is an aspect of human functioning which is as universal as language itself. Attention needs constantly to be drawn to this fact. Any possibility of intimidating with mathematical expertise is to be avoided.

(ATM)

We are committed to developing a child-centred, humanising curriculum with an internationalist perspective. We are constantly asking ourselves 'what does the child need to know' in order to be 'at home' in the world.

(NATD)

We are partners both in terms of being married and in terms of working together. We have taught together and worked in teacher education together for over 25 years. We do not however share subject backgrounds. Tony is a teacher of mathematics with a nervousness about learning and teaching through drama; Helen is a teacher of drama with a nervousness, verging on fear, of all things mathematical. We would argue that this makes us an ideal partnership to explore how we can intertwine mathematics and drama, and over the years we have explored this in many different contexts.

As active members of our respective subject associations we realized that although many people might see the subject disciplines as very different, the aims and guiding principles of the associations, two of which open this chapter, suggest that we share common beliefs about the purpose of education.

Our aim for this chapter is to offer a context for cross-curricular work in mathematics and, in particular, mathematics and drama, although we would argue it is may be more appropriate to describe it as mathematics through drama. We exemplify this approach through describing a workshop that we ran at the ATM conference in 2016.

CROSS-CURRICULAR WORK OUTSIDE THE UK

In recent years, we have found ourselves working outside the UK more and more. We ask ourselves whether there is more of an appetite for cross-curricular work outside the UK. It can feel that schools in the UK have become more focused on curriculum 'delivery' and coverage of subject specific objectives rather than exploring ways in which subject areas can collaborate. Of course, in a heavily objective-led curriculum, cross-curricular work can support us in ensuring that objectives from across disciplines are experienced in the same lesson by learners and that this could be seen as an economical way of teaching the curriculum.

Much of our work is in International Schools and many of these schools follow the International Baccalaureate (IB) programme. The IB curriculum places expectations on all teachers of the curriculum to develop a learner profile among its students. This profile asks that all students should become:

- **Inquirers**: students should develop their natural curiosity.

- **Knowledgeable**: students should explore concepts, ideas and issues that have both a local and global significance.

- **Thinkers**: students should think critically to engage themselves in figuring out complex problems.

- **Communicators**: students should express themselves and information through a variety of modes of communication.

- **Principled**: students should act honestly and with a strong sense of fairness, justice, and respect for the dignity of the individual, groups, and communities.

- **Open-minded**: students should appreciate their own cultures and personal histories and be open to the perspectives, values and traditions of other individuals and communities.

- **Caring**: students should show respect and compassion towards the needs of others.

- **Risk-takers**: students should approach unfamiliar situations with courage, as well as defend their beliefs.

- **Balanced**: students should understand the importance of intellectual, physical and emotional balance to achieve personal wellbeing.

- **Reflective:** students should give thoughtful consideration to their own learning and experience.

Something we ask of all teachers of mathematics that we work with is to reflect on how they develop this learner profile through their teaching of mathematics. We also ask them to audit their lessons against this profile and to analyse the dispositions to which they pay most attention, and those that they may not be meeting. We invite you to do the same. We would argue that cross-curricular approaches to learning and teaching mathematics offer opportunities to develop this learner profile. It was with this, and with the two guiding principles that opened the chapter in mind, that we turned our attention to planning a cross-curricular workshop for the ATM conference.

The particular idea of a humanizing curriculum with an international perspective led us to plan a workshop that would allow teachers to explore the current and continuing refugee crisis. We hoped to foreground developing open-minded and caring learners. In common with all of our workshops, we did not define objectives at the outset; it was simply entitled mathematics and drama. The objectives unfolded as we worked together:

LEARNING AS A SOCIAL ACTIVITY

Learning becomes deeply social (and sometimes personal) play because learners know that they are contracting into fiction and they understand the power they have within that fiction to direct, decide and function.

(NATD)

Teaching and learning are cooperative activities. Encouraging a questioning approach and giving due attention to the ideas of others are attitudes to be encouraged.

(ATM)

After a very brief introduction to ourselves and a brief sharing of individual backgrounds, we invited the participants, in groups of five, to engage with a series of activities that would often be more directly linked to drama, although one of the activities was developed from an ATM publication *People Mathematics* (Bloomfield and Vertes, 2005). These activities were planned in order to bring people together (literally and metaphorically) but also to begin to introduce ideas of boundaries and enclosures; of danger, safety and protection. We would claim that such activities have a place in all mathematics teaching, as the development of a community of learners supports exploration of complex ideas. We would also suggest that teachers of mathematics use such activities in mathematics lessons in order to support the development of a community of learners in mathematics. This is particularly important in secondary classrooms when teachers may only see pupils a few times a week.

ACTIVITY

Bomb and shield

This game was developed by Augustus Boal (2008) as a part of his *Theatre of the Oppressed* project. *Theatre of the Oppressed* has the explicit aim of using education to help people understand their social reality in order to change it. In this game, participants spread out around the room. Without revealing their choices, each person chooses one person in the room to be a 'bomb' and another to be their 'shield'. The aim of the game is to keep your 'shield' between you and your 'bomb' as people move around the room. There was a lot of frantic movement as we counted down from ten to one when the 'bomb' explodes.

We noted that since this game was devised by Boal, the context has become very close to real life. We now choose to introduce it as 'Aliens and defenders' when we work with young learners. In Boal's time there were no suicide bombers who would literally blow themselves up.

ACTIVITY

Touching the floor

While 'bomb and shield' introduced ideas of safety, danger and protection, the next game brought us closer together. We would shout out a number and each group, while remaining in contact with each other the whole time, had to keep this number of body parts on the floor. Ten was easy as the group simply held hands with ten feet touching the floor. For numbers greater than ten, some of the group would need to add hands, or noses, or foreheads to the floor. For numbers less than ten, individuals would have to balance, and for numbers less than five, one of the group members would need to be entirely supported.

ACTIVITY

Smallest area

Our final activity in this section invited each group to find the smallest area that they could all balance in. We asked them to mark out this area with masking tape and to calculate the area. Again, we were subtly introducing the idea of confinement and support. It also involved the groups in some estimating, measuring and calculation. Thus began the transition to mathematics.

ACTIVITY

The journey from Syria

After a brief period of reflection, we moved into the next section of the workshop and asked each group of five to make 25 miniature 'people' using modelling clay. We asked that these should be a twentieth of the average size of the individual members of each group. We left the definition of 'average' to each group and they interpreted this in a variety of ways although there was some evidence of measurement and division. We were fascinated by the care that people took in making these models, even though we had not yet told the groups what we would be using the models for.

While the participants were working on this task, they were set another problem: 'How long would it take you to walk 4320km?'

Again, we did not offer a context for this problem. As groups finished the modelling, we drew together to create a map on the floor of the space using masking tape. At this point the context for the question became clear – 4320km is the distance from the Syrian border to Calais, France. Google Maps suggests this journey would take 831 hours to walk. We agreed that this would take a minimum of three months if we included sleeping breaks and difficulties in crossing borders. The participants used the information given below to create the map.

If you are planning on using this activity in the classroom, we would suggest that you create a series of fact sheets. This information would make up the first fact sheet. You could include a wider range of countries if you had time. The distances are all taken from Google Maps. You can even download a Google Map of the journey for pupils to look at.

Distances

- Syria to Turkish border nearest Greece: 1500km
- Syria to Macedonian border: 2000km
- Syria to Austria/Germany border: 3100km
- Syria to Germany/France border: 3700km
- Syria to Calais: 4320km

Figure 11.1   Miniature people in modelling clay

(Continued)

(Continued)

The next task was to place our 100 models (there had been four groups) along the route from Syria to Calais. Each model represented one per cent of the people displaced in and from Syria as a result of the war. Another set of information (below) was needed for this task. This information was taken from the UNICEF website, and we would recommend that you use the most up-to-date information to create this fact sheet. It could even be an additional piece of research for the learners.

People displaced by the war in Syria in April 2016

The population of Syria is 22.8 million. It is estimated that 6.6 million have been displaced within the country and 4.8 million displaced to other countries. So approximately 50 per cent of the population has been displaced: 29 per cent internally and 21 per cent to other countries.

More recent estimates (June 2016) suggest the following numbers of refugees in selected countries:

- Turkey 2.8 million
- Lebanon 1.5 million
- Jordan 1.5 million
- Germany 500 000
- Macedonia 400 000
- France 10 000
- UK 8000
- the numbers of refugees in the camps in Dunkirk and Calais total approximately 6000.

As the figures were placed onto the map the atmosphere changed, and there was a real sense of not wanting to put the figures in danger. We realized the extent to which the participants had contracted 'into fiction and they understand the power they have within that fiction to direct, decide and function' (NATD) and we had clearly found ways to meet the requirements of another guiding principle of ATM:

> The power to learn rests with the learner. Teaching has a subordinate role. The teacher has a duty to seek out ways to engage the power of the learner.

The final act for the group was to place the English Channel on the map. The group calculated that this was the width of one of the tape measures we had been using to measure out the scaled distances. One participant looked back at the image of the journey, with our models spread out along the journey and said, 'if you had come all that way, of course you are going to try and get over the Channel'.

The activity had also modelled very clearly the tiny proportion of Syrian refugees that have reached the Channel. The 6000 people in the camps at Dunkirk and Calais were represented by 0.1 per cent of a person (an arm), with a finger representing the refugees who had successfully and safely reached the UK.

Figure 11.2   Map of the journey from Syria to Calais

The final section of the workshop moved on to introduce a drama technique called 'The Mantle of the Expert'. This also allowed us to model ways of supporting learners in becoming active, in changing their world through coming to an increased understanding of the world.

MANTLE OF THE EXPERT

The idea of the 'Mantle of the Expert' was developed by Dorothy Heathcote and is described as a dramatic-inquiry based approach to teaching and learning. The big idea is that the class do all their curriculum work as if they are an imagined group of experts (Heathcote and Bolton, 1995; MoE).

When engaging in a 'mantle', learners take on responsibility for running an enterprise in a fictional world. This role is developed sufficiently so that they care enough about the long-term goals of the fictional client to engage in activities through which they begin to imagine the fictional world that they have been presented with. Learners and teachers together: interact predominantly as themselves while imagining that they are interacting as experts; imagine that they are interacting as other people in the fictional world. Over time, learners engage with activities that are at the same time curriculum tasks, although they appear as professional practices in the fictional enterprise. In any 'mantle' the teacher must share power to position the students (individually and collectively) as knowledgeable and competent colleagues.

ACTIVITY

Social enterprise

The 'enterprise' that Helen introduced was a business that recycled shipping containers for a range of other uses. Drawing on images of actual uses for old shipping containers, she showed how the fictional business had supported the creation of pop-up shops in Shoreditch, London,

(Continued)

(Continued)

and worked to create shelters for the homeless in Brighton. In her role as Chief Executive Officer of the charity she told the group that the charity had decided to take a new direction. She read out the following 'letter' that she had received from a boy in a local primary school. He had written this letter as a result of a visit to the school by UNICEF to talk about the plight of child refugees. The letter is reproduced below. When working with children we would use a handwritten letter that could be passed around the groups.

We are writing because we are very sad. Children like us are dying in the sea. We saw it on TV. Children cannot get to go to school. We want to help. Somebody left an old container on the road near our school. We think it would make an amazing classroom for our friends in Calais. Will came to talk to us from UNICEF and we do not like what is happening at all. Please help us make a nice warm fun place for them to learn like us.

Helen then described how she had become inspired by this letter to reform the business as a social enterprise that would recycle shipping containers. The shipping containers would be transformed into mobile classrooms that could be transported to any area of the world where children were being deprived of education. The participants were invited to become a member of one of the following teams. Individuals made their own choices of role by selecting a role card labelled with the particular job they were volunteering for:

- accountancy team
- US offices team
- marketing team
- Asian offices team
- donor negotiations and communications team
- design team.

New groups were formed that contained a number of these roles. Individuals introduced themselves, explaining what skills and experiences they had that had led them to make this choice.

Figure 11.3   Developing a company logo

This is the point at which individuals could decide how much of a character they wanted to create and inhabit. Once the groups had introduced themselves, they discussed a name and a logo for the social enterprise. After sharing and discussing, the logo and name shown in Fig. 11.3 was adopted.

The final activity for the session involved the groups working with shoe boxes as scale models of containers. The shoe boxes were about $\frac{1}{20}$ of the size of a shipping container so the groups picked up their figures from the scale map at the back of the room and placed them in the classrooms they had constructed.

Figure 11.4   Model of the container classroom

CLOSING THOUGHTS

Munir Fasheh (2016) challenged readers to think of learning and assessment through new eyes. He defined the Arabic word *mujaawarah* as a personal and communal freedom to learn and act in harmony with wellbeing and wisdom. We spent a moment thinking of how often such a freedom exists in our mathematics classrooms and whether or not these activities had offered us personal and communal freedom to learn and act in harmony with wellbeing and wisdom. In the same article Fasheh redefined assessment in terms of an Arabic term *yuhsen*. *Yuhsen* is a combination of one's performance in action and one's relationship to who and what is around, and offers an alternative view of assessment. For Fasheh, a person's worth is judged by looking at the interconnectivity of:

- how well they use a skill

- the beauty of the outcomes

- how useful the outcomes are to the community

- how respectfully the process is engaged in

- the humility of the act.

We used these statements to reflect on and evaluate the previous three hours. Our final thought took us back to both the value of cross-curricular work and to the importance of collaboration across disciplines.

Beyond right and wrong there is a field; I will meet you there.

(Fasheh, 2016: 9)

REFERENCES

ATM (Association of Teachers of Mathematics) Guiding Principles. Available at: https://www.atm.org.uk/ATM-aims-principles.

Bloomfield, **A** and **Vertes**, **B** (2005) *People Maths: Hidden Depths*. Derby: ATM. Available at: https://www.atm.org.uk/Shop/People-Maths-Hidden-Depths---PDF/dnl014

Boal, **A** (2008) *Theatre of the Oppressed*. London: Pluto Press.

Fasheh, **M** (2016) 'Over 68 years with mathematics: Part 2', *Mathematics Teaching*, 251: 7-10.

Heathcote, **D** and **Bolton**, **G** (1995) *Drama for Learning: Dorothy Heathcote's Mantle of the Expert Approach to Education*. Portsmouth, NH: Heinemann USA.

IB (International Baccalaureate) learner profile. Available at: http://www.ibo.org/globalassets/publications/recognition/learnerprofile-en.pdf. Accessed 13.6.16.

MoE (Mantle of the Expert) A dramatic-inquiry approach to teaching and learning. Available at: http://www.mantleoftheexpert.com.

NATD (National Association for the Teaching of Drama) Guiding Principles. Available at:http://www.natd.eu/.

UNICEF, Refugee Situations. Available at: http://data.unhcr.org/syrianrefugees/regional.php.

Author's note: a previous version of this chapter has appeared in *Mathematics Teaching 264*, published by the Association of Teachers of Mathematics.

12
USING THE HISTORY OF MATHEMATICS

SUE POPE

┌─────────────── **IN THIS CHAPTER** ───────────────┐

This chapter:

- explores the potential of themes from history in the teaching of mathematics
- develops activities that focus on the challenge of history
- helps children to ask questions.

└──┘

Mathematics has a fascinating history from across the world. The cultural and historical roots of mathematics can build children's interest in mathematics and contribute to developing a positive attitude towards the subject. Learning that mathematics is part of human development over time and all around the world is a testament to human ingenuity. Mathematics has developed in tandem with the evolution of human civilization. Managing society has presented problems and challenges for which mathematics provides the tools for resolution.

The benefits of using the history of mathematics in the classroom are well documented in an ICMI study (Fauvel and van Maanen, 2000). Its use:

- enhances mathematical learning
- exposes the nature of mathematics and mathematical activity

- enriches teacher's understanding and pedagogic approach

- promotes an affective predisposition towards mathematics

- reveals mathematics as a cultural human endeavour.

It can provide:

- starting points for children to ask their own questions (inquiry-based learning, philosophy for children)

- a means for making links with other aspects of the curriculum: citizenship, geography, history, science, art and design, design and technology

- opportunities for connecting different mathematical ideas.

Of course, there are arguments against using the history of mathematics in an overcrowded curriculum. It may be considered to be 'not mathematics', confusing, irrelevant and boring. There may be a lack of time, resources and expertise. As it is not assessed, it is not valued.

If you are looking for ways that mathematics can contribute to children's spiritual, moral, social and cultural education, then the history of mathematics has a great deal to offer. In our increasingly globalized pluralist society, appreciation of mathematics as a human endeavour with roots in China, India, the Middle East, Africa and South America challenges the white male Eurocentric view of mathematics so often perpetuated through the school curriculum. Mathematics is neither culture- nor value-free. Not including the history of mathematics denies children the opportunity to know the ubiquity of mathematics throughout human development.

The activities in this chapter aim to provide accessible starting points that support understanding of school mathematics as well as developing the whole person. They lend themselves to group work and communication of findings via presentations and/or posters.

ACTIVITY

Ancient number systems

Resources

You will need copies of the Babylonian and Egyptian number systems and possibly calculators so that calculations do not get in the way of creative thinking.

Useful links

- Robson, E. (n.d.) Babylonian Maths, https://motivate.maths.org/content/BabylonianMaths

- NRICH, http://nrich.maths.org/6853&part= http://nrich.maths.org/6908.

National curriculum and mathematical understanding links

Suitable for: age 8 and above.

Objectives: to explore ancient number systems and consider similarities and differences; to appreciate place value and the arbitrariness of base.

Mathematical understanding: place value; conversion between different representations; considering 'where does mathematics come from?'; different methods for multiplying.

Setting the scene

Ask children where they think mathematics comes from. What about the numbers we use? Does everyone use the same system of numbers? You may be fortunate to have children in your class from different parts of the world – if not, you could show artefacts with Arabic, Indian, Chinese, etc. numerals. A map helps children see how ideas come from around the world. The significance of the silk trade routes for the sharing and development of ideas including mathematics becomes clear when looking at a world map.

We know about the way Babylonians recorded numbers and other information because they wrote in clay with a stylus. The stylus had two ends that made two different marks, and the clay was left to dry in the sun so the tablet could be preserved for a long time.

Children may have seen pottery fragments during a museum visit. Invite children to work in groups and decipher the Babylonian numbers in Figure 12.1. This copy of a clay tablet shows multiples of nine – this should help children to decide which symbols represent 'one' and 'ten', for example, by seeing that 18 is 'one ten' and 'eight ones'.

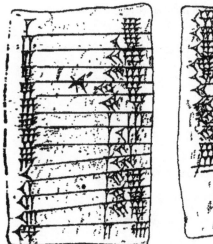 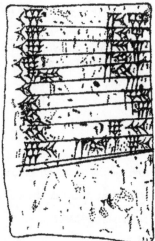

Figure 12.1   Babylonian clay tablet (1800 BCE) showing multiples of nine

(Continued)

(Continued)

When the children get to the seventh row, they may be surprised to see the symbols for 'one' and 'three'. This is because the Babylonians used place value, as we do, where the digits represent different amounts depending on where they are placed. For example, we use a system where 10 means 'one ten' and 1000 means 'one thousand'. The Babylonians used a place value system base 60 for numbers greater than 59, so the 'one' in this seventh-row entry on the clay tablet represents 'one sixty' and 'three ones'.

The Egyptians had a very different system of numbers. They used a different symbol for each power of ten (the Babylonians did this for one and ten and then used place value).

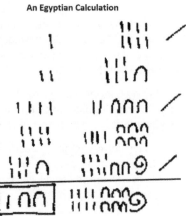

An Egyptian Calculation

Decimal Number	Egyptian Symbol	What it represents
1		staff
10		heel bone
100		coil of rope
1000		lotus flower
10 000		pointing finger
100 000		tadpole
1 000 000		astonished man

Figure 12.2   Egyptian number system and calculation

Provide children with a copy of the symbols and calculations so they can 'play detective' and decide what calculation is being carried out and how.

Trigger questions

- What are the multiples of nine?
- What do the symbols mean?
- Why is the seventh multiple of nine written 'one three'?
- What does it mean to have place value base 60?
- Why might 60 be chosen as a base?
- Is base 60 used today?
- How does the Babylonian number system compare with the Hindu-Arabic numbers we use today?
- What is the greatest multiple of nine on the clay tablet?
- How does the Egyptian system for numbers compare with the Babylonian system?

- What method did the Egyptians use for multiplying?

- How might you adapt this approach for division?

Review and reflect

Ask children to write some numbers using the Egyptian and Babylonian systems (for example, age, house number, year of birth, etc.). Which system is easier to use and why? Why do we use a place value system? Complete a multiplication using the Egyptian method. Explain why the method works.

Assessment

Children can check their work using alternative calculation strategies.

Are children able to explain how place value works and appreciate that the base is immaterial as long as it used consistently, for example, base ten the places are ones (10^0), tens (10^1), hundreds (10^2), ... ; base 60 the places are ones (60^0), sixties (60^1), three thousand six hundreds (60^2), ...?

Can children extend the Egyptian method of multiplication to division?

Follow-up tasks

Children could research how fractions were represented in the different number systems. They could investigate other ancient number systems, for example, Mayans used base 20.

ACTIVITY

Florence Nightingale

Resources

You will need copies of Florence Nightingale's Coxcomb diagrams and the use of laptop computers.

Useful links

- Open University (OU) TV programme and other clips about Florence Nightingale: https://www.youtube.com/watch?v=yhXOOR1_Vfc

- Science News animation of the coxcomb and bar chart: https://www.sciencenews.org/pictures/mathtrek/112608/nightingale.swf

- Understanding uncertainty: https://understandinguncertainty.org/coxcombs

- University of York: https://www.york.ac.uk/depts/maths/histstat/small.htm

- United Nations (UN): http://www.undp.org/content/undp/en/home/sustainable-development-goals/

- Global Issues: www.globalissues.org/article/26/poverty-facts-and-stats

- Gapminder: www.gapminder.org.

(Continued)

(Continued)

National curriculum and mathematical understanding links

Suitable for: age 9 and above.

Objectives: to consider how data can be used to persuade and convince; to explore different representations of data and why they might be helpful; to use spreadsheets to display data.

Mathematical understanding: using statistics for a purpose, representing and interpreting data.

Setting the scene

Ask children whether they have ever heard of Florence Nightingale. What do they know about her? Nightingale (1820-1910) is often depicted as a nurse but, more importantly, she was a statistician who used data to persuade people to make changes. You might like to show the short OU video – see 'Resources' above. During the Crimean War (1853-56) Nightingale collected data about the cause of soldiers' deaths. She illustrated the data on diagrams, making a strong case for better hygiene in hospitals to result in fewer deaths from contagious (zymotic) diseases. The Sanitary Commission arrived in March 1855 to improve conditions.

Florence used the annual mortality rate per 1000 soldiers in her diagrams. For example, in July 1854, there were 28 772 soldiers and 359 died from contagious disease (that is, their death had nothing to do with being in battle). If the same rate of death had occurred over one year, that would be 12×359 deaths, and as there were 28 772 soldiers and a rate per 1000 is needed, the calculation is:

$$\frac{12 \times 359 \times 1000}{28722} = 150.0 \text{ to 1d.p.}$$

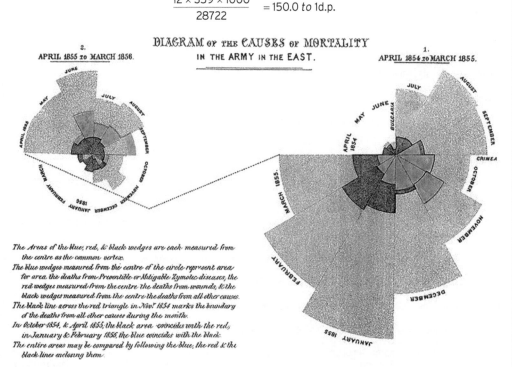

Figure 12.3   Diagram showing the mortality rate per 1000 soldiers during the Crimean War

The diagram is not easy to analyse as the area of the sectors represent the mortality rate per 1000 soldiers and there were different numbers of soldiers in Crimea at different times. The data for the years 1854-56 is summarized in Table 12.1.

Table 12.1   Summary of data for mortality rate per 100 soldiers during the years 1854-56

Month	Average size of army	Annual rate of mortality per 1000		
		Zymotic diseases	Wounds & injuries	All other causes
Apr 1854	8571	1.4	0.0	7.0
May 1854	23333	6.2	0.0	4.6
Jun 1854	28333	4.7	0.0	2.5
Jul 1854	28722	150.0	0.0	9.6
Aug 1854	30246	328.5	0.4	11.9
Sep 1854	30290	312.2	32.1	27.7
Oct 1854	30643	197.0	51.7	50.1
Nov 1854	29736	340.6	115.8	42.8
Dec 1854	32779	631.5	41.7	48.0
Jan 1855	32393	1022.8	30.7	120.0
Feb 1855	30919	822.8	16.3	140.1
Mar 1855	30107	480.3	12.8	68.6
Apr 1855	32252	177.5	17.9	21.2
May 1855	35473	171.8	16.6	12.5
Jun 1855	38863	247.6	64.5	9.6
Jul 1855	42647	107.5	37.7	9.3
Aug 1855	44614	129.9	44.1	6.7
Sep 1855	47751	47.5	69.4	5.0
Oct 1855	46852	32.8	13.6	4.6
Nov 1855	37853	56.4	10.5	10.1
Dec 1855	43217	25.3	5.0	7.8
Jan 1856	44212	11.4	0.5	13.0
Feb 1856	43485	6.6	0.0	5.2
Mar 1856	46140	3.9	0.0	9.1

Use a spreadsheet to explore different representations of this data.

(Continued)

(Continued)

Trigger questions

- What does the diagram show?

- Why are there three different colours?

- What was the most likely cause of death?

- Why did Florence use an annual rate per 1000 soldiers? Could she have used other rates?

- In March 1855, the sanitary commission visited the war hospital. Do you think the visit made a differ-ence? Why?

- What representation would you recommend to Florence Nightingale? Why?

Review and reflect

Florence Nightingale used statistics to make a case for change. Why did she use diagrams to help do this? What sort of diagrams can be used to compare data like Florence Nightingale's on a spreadsheet? Children can work in groups to create a display with an explanation for their choice of representation and its interpretation.

Assessment

Children's explanations demonstrate understanding of the statistics used and why a mortality rate per 1000 was used rather than just the raw number of deaths. Children can manipulate charts on a spreadsheet and justify their choices.

Follow-up tasks

- Children could research Florence Nightingale's ongoing crusade for better health care in England throughout her life - see University of York under 'Useful links' above. The UN's sustainable develop-ment goals are monitored through the collection of statistics and include global health - see United Nations under 'Useful links' above.

- Many organizations have a wealth of international statistics - see Global Issues under 'Useful links' above.

- Gapminder (see 'Useful links' above) represents world data in a highly visual way that can inspire chil-dren to engage with statistics. Children could work in groups to research an issue of their choice and prepare a poster or presentation for the rest of the class.

ACTIVITY

Systematizing geometry

Resources

You will need linking polygons, for example, Polydron, Clixi, ATM MATs.

National curriculum and mathematical understanding links

Suitable for: age 7 and above.

Objectives: to explore Platonic and Archimedean solids and regular and semi-regular tessellations.

Mathematical understanding: properties of shape; angle sum of a triangle; interior angles; creating 3D shapes from regular polygons; creating tessellations from regular polygons; nets of polyhedra creating arguments to justify findings.

Setting the scene

Provide a large collection of practical resources for making 3D shapes. What shapes can be made if there must be the same number of regular polygons meeting at each vertex?

Encourage children to work systematically: for example, start with equilateral triangles:

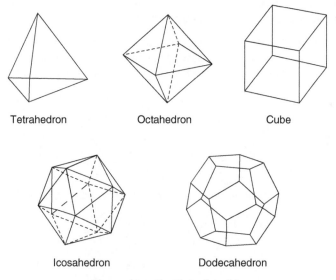

Tetrahedron   Octahedron   Cube

Icosahedron   Dodecahedron

Figure 12.4   The Platonic solids

Three triangles at a vertex gives the tetrahedron, four the octahedron, five the icosahedron and six triangles at a vertex is flat – why? Solids made from identical equilateral triangles are known as deltahedra – the geodesic dome and buckyball are examples. For a square, three at a vertex gives a cube and four is flat – why? For a pentagon, three at a vertex gives the dodecahedron. For a hexagon, three at a vertex is flat.

These five regular polyhedra are the only ones that satisfy the conditions (the same number and type of regular polygons that meet at each vertex). Known to the Greeks, they are called the Platonic solids. Euclid's *Elements Book XIII* was devoted to these solids. Children can count the faces, vertices and edges of the solids and notice the relationships between the results.

(Continued)

(Continued)

The three 'flat' combinations form the regular tessellations.

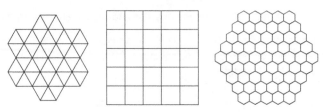

Figure 12.5   The regular tessellations

The regular tessellations can be used to determine the interior angles of an equilateral triangle, square and regular hexagon. The angle sum of a triangle is 180°; this fact can be used to determine the size of the interior angle in any regular polygon, by finding out the minimum number of triangles that the polygon can be divided into. This gives the angle sum of the polygon, which can be divided by the number of sides to give the interior angle of the regular polygon.

Discuss with children what shapes can be made if you can use more than one type of regular polygon and the vertices must be identical? This investigation will result in the discovery of semi-regular polyhedra, the 13 Archimedean solids, whose names alone will cause children considerable delight:

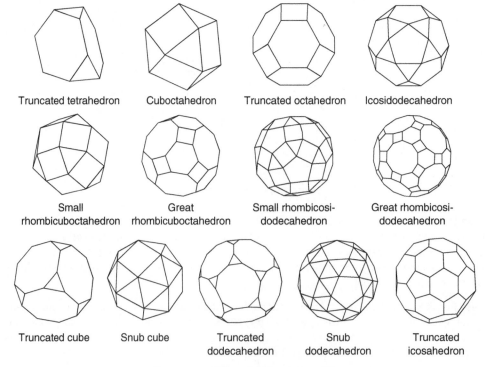

Figure 12.6   The 13 Archimedean solids

It will also reveal two infinite families, that is:

- prisms made from two regular *n*-sided polygons and *n* squares

- anti-prisms made from two regular *n*-sided polygons and *n* equilateral triangles. The octahedron is a triangular based antiprism.

It will also give eight semi-regular tessellations known as the Archimedean tilings:

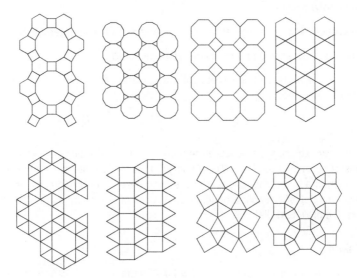

Figure 12.7   Archimedean tilings

Archimedes (approximately 250 BCE) lived somewhat later than Euclid (approximately 400 BCE) and was a highly inventive mathematician and scientist.

Trigger questions

- Why are there only five Platonic solids?

- Why are some combinations of regular polygons flat?

- What is the angle sum of the polygons at a vertex?

- What is the interior angle of a square, equilateral triangle, regular hexagon?

- What is the minimum number of triangles that a pentagon can be cut into? What about other polygons?

- Will the angle sum of a pentagon always be the same?

- What is the interior angle of a regular pentagon?

- Can you extend these ideas to other polygons?

- Can you draw the net for one of your solids?

(Continued)

(Continued)

- How many vertices, edges and faces are there? Is there a connection between them?
- Can you draw and colour a tessellation on a computer?

Review and reflect

What is a regular polygon?

What is a regular polyhedron?

What is the difference between a regular tessellation and a semi-regular tessellation?

How many different nets can you find for a cube (for example)?

What is true about the angle sum at a vertex of a tessellation and how is it different to the angle sum at a vertex of a polyhedron?

Assessment

Children can work systematically to ensure they have all possible solids and tessellations, and can devise a means of recording their findings. Children are able to distinguish between regular and semi-regular polyhedra and tessellations. Children can determine the interior angle of a regular polygon and use this to justify angle properties of vertices of polyhedra and tessellations. Children can create nets and draw tessellations.

Follow-up tasks

Children could research the Platonic solids, Euclid's Elements and the Archimedean solids and tilings (semi-regular tessellations). They may want to investigate geodesic domes in the world, for example, the Eden Project in Cornwall. Creating the tessellations using computer software and exploring different ways of colouring them will produce fabulous classroom displays.

REFERENCES

Fauvel, J and **van Maanen, JA** (eds) (2000) *History in Mathematics Education: An ICMI Study.* Dordrecht: Springer Netherlands.

FURTHER READING

Joseph, GG (1991) *The Crest of the Peacock: Non-European Roots of Mathematics.* London: IB Tauris.

Katz, V (2007) *The Mathematics of Egypt, Mesopotamia, China, India and Islam.* New Jersey. Princeton University Press.

Katz, V and **Parshall, KH** (2014) *Taming the Unknown: History of Algebra from Antiquity to the Early Twentieth Century.* Princeton and Oxford: Princeton University Press.

13
MATHEMATICS AND HOME

JOSH LURY

┌─────────── **IN THIS CHAPTER** ───────────┐

This chapter:

- highlights the importance of home-school links
- considers the importance of children's mathematical identity
- explores how children begin to use mathematics from birth
- considers the mathematical learning environment
- looks beyond arithmetic across a range of mathematics.

└──┘

MATHEMATICAL SELF-ESTEEM

The ideas in this chapter are relevant for all learners but may be particularly beneficial for those who lack mathematical esteem and who may experience anxiety and even fear in mathematics lessons. The activities offered in this chapter have been designed to be used as part of a home-school link, and require very little preparation from the teacher, very little in the way of explanation, but could make a profound difference to the way children think of themselves as mathematicians.

Building a sense of your own worth as a mathematician takes more than just being told to face the challenges, or being given a visual or concrete resource to support your thinking. It takes experience of success and of overcoming obstacles. More than just getting the right answer, it requires seeing why your answer has meaning and appreciating how your solution makes sense in the real world.

Changing someone's identity as a mathematician is far from easy. Once someone has decided they are 'no good at maths', every mathematics lesson will be a trial, and anxiety may be accompanied by disengagement or boredom. Making a difference for such learners can feel very difficult, but there are some things worth trying. The classroom is not necessarily the best place to start as habitual practices may be too strong, but the home offers an environment rich in mathematical talk and opportunity.

MATHEMATICS IN THE HOME

Children learn their earliest mathematics in the home. Babies' brains are hard-wired for pattern recognition, both visual and auditory. Parents and carers engage in baby talk, in which the rhythms and intonations of speech are exaggerated and even formalized in nursery rhymes. Furthermore, children develop a number of 'natural powers' (Mason, 2005) that are inherently mathematical, that they can use in mathematical learning. The 'powers' are in pairs, namely:

- imagine and express

- organize and classify

- conjecture and convince

- generalize and specialize.

The terms 'conjecture' and 'generalize' sound like technical mathematical terms, but given a short consideration, it is clear that children learn and employ these skills at home, before they even begin schooling. A child lining up her toys, deciding which toy cars to park together, which teddies are placed on the floor and which on the pillow, will be sorting based on properties, and will be able to express the reasons for her decisions, will determine general rules about which toys can or cannot be used in certain ways. A child refusing to eat pasta with tomato sauce may conjecture that they will not like it because of the sauce, or some other generalization about red foods, and will certainly aim to convince their family that their decisions are based on sound reasons and will employ detailed logic.

Without doubt, these 'natural powers' are used and developed in the home, through experience and experimentation, and through interaction with parents and carers, and it is these very powers that a professional mathematician uses daily in pursuit even of the most highly abstract mathematics. Carers, parents and grandparents use these powers all the time as well – they are natural modes of thinking, and people use them intuitively and with great flexibility both in their working lives and in the day-to-day habits of living. Yet, many feel they have little to offer their child in terms of mathematics education, and will say to their child's teacher, 'I was never any good at maths'. You hear it said variously with fear or bravado, without hope or expectation, with resignation and without interest. Perhaps mathematics is one of the hardest of subjects to learn, yet in other countries and cultures, children tend to have much greater success and everyone is believed capable of learning mathematics.

MATHEMATICS AS MORE THAN ARITHMETIC

In the UK, mathematics is feared by many, considered too cold and austere to understand or enjoy, and this fear is passed down the generations. We can guess at the causes of this perception – generations of people taught mathematics without understanding, without a sense that there are comprehensible and even beautiful patterns that we can all get to grips with; dry, abstract subject matter; and plenty of dull, repetitive practice. We need to build bridges and change how mathematics is perceived and how people perceive themselves as mathematicians. To change these perceptions, we need to invite the children and their families to the table.

There may be some barriers and some misconceptions to tackle, in order to make the attempt authentic and genuinely helpful. One of the most common perceptions is that mathematics is, essentially, arithmetic, and that learning more in mathematics means being able to calculate with larger numbers more quickly. In this chapter, the home-based activities are designed to develop an interest in mathematics that is more than arithmetic, that forefront deeper and more intuitive mathematical thinking, such as Mason's 'powers', and that recognize the importance of fostering mathematical talk and mathematical learning in the home, highlighting that parents and carers are children's primary educators. Before children come to school they have already learnt a great deal largely alone but also with the stimulus and support of others in the home.

The activities are designed to show that arithmetic is just a part of mathematics but is certainly not the primary form that mathematics can take. Each activity prompts talk about mathematical thinking, rather than anxiety about 'getting the answer right', and all the activities are designed to connect mathematics with the real world. To strengthen the link between home and school, it may be very effective to invite parents and carers to school before and after the activities, to discuss the richness of the mathematical learning that can happen even without drill and practice. The major incentive for these activities is to bring mathematics to life, to create a sense of joy and bring a sensory and cognitive richness to the subject.

Each activity is easily adaptable to suit your class, with a little thought about the appropriate level of challenge, or the numbers involved:

- **If ...** - using prediction to develop strategy and deduction - this activity motivates through the use of simple strategy games, helps demonstrate how mathematical thinking skills come quite naturally in context, and develops logical reasoning through the sentence stem 'If this happens then ...'.

- **Testing conjectures** - using mathematics to model the world, and making conjectures, showing 'it is ok to be wrong'.

- **Humans vs. technology** - harnessing the brain's capacity to spot patterns, and to build esteem through becoming 'faster than a calculator'.

- **Measured baking challenge** - using a range of measurement skills to employ mathematics in a practical and sensory context.

ACTIVITY

If ...

Resources

Dice, pencil and paper

(Continued)

(Continued)

Curriculum and mathematical understanding links

Suitable for: age 7-11.

Objectives: to recognize deep mathematical thinking skills; to develop the use of prediction; to prompt mathematical discussions in the home and at school.

Setting the scene

Prediction is a vital mathematical skill that, combined with estimation and approximation, forms very useful checking skills, prompting reasoning over guesswork.

Strategic thinking and logical reasoning are vital problem-solving skills, and necessary for building a deeper understanding of efficient use of mathematics.

Sharing a game with family and discussing the tactics prompts mathematical discussions that are about logic and reasoning, and demonstrate that mathematics is much more than arithmetic.

Dice prediction

Play a game with the class of rolling one dice and predicting the score. You get five points if your guess is exactly right, and one point if your guess is one away.

Discuss how to keep score (a tally chart is suitable for this task, or collecting counters to keep the total), and play against the class.

Roll ten times each and compare scores at the end. Discuss who made the best predictions, and whether there was any luck involved.

Now play the game with two dice, with the aim to predict the total of both dice. Discuss how the predictions will change, and what has changed. After a few rounds, those that notice 6, 7 and 8 are far more likely scores will be making far better predictions.

Strategy and prediction

Now play a simple pencil and paper game – Noughts and Crosses works perfectly.

This time, instead of predicting what an object will do, the task is to predict what your opponent will do. The teacher can model this thinking process by voicing decision-making processes such as 'If I go here, then you will go there'.

Notice how making predictions can help you win more often, as it allows you to adjust your tactics, and avoid falling into traps set by your opponent.

Play a strategy game at home. Use your powers of prediction to improve your tactics. Be ready to share your tactics with the class.

Set children the task of playing a strategy game with their family. In Chapter 7, there are descriptions of games such as Nim, so children could be given choice about the game to play. Some families may have access to board or strategy games in the home, such as Connect Four. However, to make sure the task is accessible to everyone, make sure to demonstrate the option of a simple pencil and paper game such as:

- Noughts and Crosses
- Dots and Squares
- Nim
- Four-in-a-row.

Set children the task of playing the games, but at the same time try to harness their ability to predict and use reasons. Suggest they try to keep the phrase 'If this happens then …' in their minds as they play, and start developing their own tactics.

Encourage the children to discuss their tactics with their opponents, and to collect the tactics of various family members. They may discover, for example, that one person always starts in the middle square, but another starts in the corner. Children should try to find out if there is a reason for these decisions, or if it is just based on a feeling or a 'hunch'.

Trigger questions

- What do you notice about your predictions and the actual number rolled?
- What do you notice about your predictions now that you are playing with one dice?
- What numbers are you more likely to roll? So, have you changed your predictions?
- Where is your opponent going to place his/her nought or cross?
- Can you explain why your opponent made such a move?
- Can you predict your opponent's next move? Why? How do you know?

Review and reflect

Back in class, reinforce the learning and notice misconceptions. Share the tactics that children have developed, and that they have learned from their families.

Children could work in groups on different games – teaching each other the new tactics and putting them to the test by playing against one another. See if they can decide which tactics are based on sound reasoning, and which seem to be nothing more than superstition.

The most important learning will come from having to explain and test the reasons behind the predictions and strategies. Return to the original dice game: there was very little strategy involved, and so the actual reasoning involved was quite limited. Compare the various strategies with the task of guessing the result of a coin-toss, which is little more than guesswork.

Assessment

Children can express and articulate the tactics they used.

Children can explain the most efficient tactic they used.

Children can explain and reason about their opponent's next move.

(Continued)

(Continued)

Follow-up tasks

- Develop your own rules for a strategy game; for example, playing Noughts and Crosses on a four-by-four grid. Teach the game to your family and see if different people can explain their new tactics.

- Research paper-and-pencil games and be ready to teach some classmates how to play.

- Play Noughts and Crosses against yourself. See if you can discover the best move to begin a game.

ACTIVITY

Testing conjectures

Resources

- list of phrases to be used as 'scaffolds'

- pencil and paper to keep a record of the conjectures collected.

Useful links

Clay Mathematics Institute (CMI): http://www.claymath.org/millennium-problems

National curriculum and mathematical understanding links

Suitable for: age 5 and above.

Objectives: to formulate and pursue lines of inquiry; to learn how mathematics models the real world.

The numbers and calculations that we use are a very efficient and unambiguous way of describing the world around us. When a learner solves the problem 'How many shoes are there in the hallway for a family of two adults and four children?' Using the calculation '6 × 2', each part of the calculation has meaning in the context given. The '6' is the total of two adults and four children, the '×' represents that each person has the same number of feet, and the '2' stands for the number of shoes per person.

The idea that numbers and symbols have some meaning based on representing the world is a very important and oft-missed step in learning about problem-solving.

Setting the scene

Begin by making a claim about the school, such as: 'there are more windows than doors in this school'.

Explain that this is your own conjecture, which means an idea you think is true, but which you have not proved. Discuss how to check the conjecture. This may include: splitting up the task for different members of the group, methods for recording the information as it is collected, and how to collate and compare the results.

Make a note of at least two different approaches, and then encourage discussion about which seems the more accurate and/or the more efficient. Once the class has debated and agreed, the conjecture can be tested, and will be either proved or disproved.

Collect a set of conjectures to investigate about your house/street/garden, by asking members of your family, then collect the information you need to check your conjectures.

Encourage children to use the word 'conjecture' with their family, and to generate the ideas by using the following scaffolds:

I think:

- there are more _____than _____
- there are fewer _____than _____
- there are twice as many _____ as _____
- there are half as many _____ as _____
- there are ten times as many _____ as _____
- there is an even number of _____
- there is an odd number of _____
- there are more than 100 _____
- there are more than 50 but fewer than 100 _____.

The children should collect the conjectures from different members of their family, and then test their veracity by collecting, recording and refining the ideas. Before revealing the answer to the family member who made the conjecture, they should discuss the reasons that the person had for making the claim.

Trigger questions

- What is your conjecture?
- How can you prove your conjecture?
- What method/strategy helped you prove your conjecture?
- Explain your reason/s for your claim.

Review and reflect

Share and compare different conjectures collected from various homes, then discuss the techniques that children used to gather data, and how they were able to decide whether the conjecture was true or false.

(Continued)

(Continued)

The most important learning is noticing how mathematics can be used to model the world around them, and that the numbers and calculations gain meaning based on the context. Discuss what children noticed and if any findings surprised them in any way.

Assessment

Back in class ask children to share the conjectures they looked at with their family.

Children can explain their conjectures and their family's.

Children are able to explain the reason behind the conjecture.

Children are able to collect the data to check the conjecture.

Children can confidently explain what a conjecture is.

Follow-up tasks

Share with children the establishment of the Millennium Prize Problems by the Clay Mathematics Institute (CMI) and how the first person to solve any of the seven problems will be awarded $1 000 000. Ask children to research one of the problems (see CMI in 'Useful links' above) solved or still unsolved.

ACTIVITY

Humans vs. technology: the power of noticing patterns

Resources

Pen and paper, patterns like the list of calculations provided below and a calculator.

National curriculum and mathematical understanding links

Suitable for: age 7 and above.

Objectives: to understand the power of pattern spotting.

Mathematical understanding: technology has become ubiquitous in the home, and it is understandable that people might argue against learning arithmetic when computers, phones and calculators can perform number-crunching tasks with a greater degree of accuracy and computational speed than any human.

Setting the scene

Write patterns such as the following on the board. Explain that the children are going to complete the calculations using a calculator.

13 × 0.1	13 ÷ 0.1	23 × 0.1	23 ÷ 0.1
14 × 0.1	14 ÷ 0.1	24 × 0.1	24 ÷ 0.1
15 × 0.1	15 ÷ 0.1	25 × 0.1	25 ÷ 0.1
16 × 0.1	16 ÷ 0.1	26 × 0.1	26 ÷ 0.1
17 × 0.1	17 ÷ 0.1	27 × 0.1	27 ÷ 0.1

Ask the children if they used the calculator for the whole time, or whether their brains worked even faster. Did you become faster than the calculator?

Give children calculation patterns to investigate. Encourage them to challenge a member of their family – one person uses a calculator to work through the lists, and the other uses their brain to try to overtake the machine.

15 × 0.2	15 ÷ 0.2	20 × 0.5	20 ÷ 0.5
20 × 0.2	20 ÷ 0.2	30 × 0.5	30 ÷ 0.5
25 × 0.2	25 ÷ 0.2	40 × 0.5	40 ÷ 0.5
30 × 0.2	30 ÷ 0.2	50 × 0.5	50 ÷ 0.5
35 × 0.2	35 ÷ 0.2	60 × 0.5	60 ÷ 0.5

Encourage children to discuss the patterns they find, and to discuss what it is about their brain that helps them complete these calculations faster than a calculator. Families will hopefully begin to have discussions about why the patterns appear, and this can also be followed up in school.

Why set this for homework instead of in class? In class, using a calculator might feel like 'cheating', and someone will no doubt get there first or say out loud 'Oh, I see' or 'This is easy', before everyone has had a chance to make that discovery. That first hint of the thought 'there are patterns here, patterns I can use' is worth hundreds of ticks or right-answers. The task is a simple one; it needs to be nothing more than a few lines written down, but the outcome is the subtle shift that might help build positive attitudes.

Trigger questions

- What patterns do you notice?

- Describe the pattern/s you see.

- Will you be faster than the calculator?

Review and reflect

There is potential for the understanding to become lost if the reasons for the patterns are not fully explored. In the case of the effects of multiplying and dividing by 0.1, children should not simply remember that 'dividing by 0.1 is the same as multiplying by 10', but must then be guided through exploring why this is the case. This could be a valuable lesson in its own right, using cubes to represent 0.1, perhaps, and framing 13 ÷ 0.1 as, 'How many 0.1s are there in 13?' Linking the manipulative model with a number line and the abstract calculation may help children

(Continued)

(Continued)

cement the links. Understanding can be strengthened further by making a real-world match, such as, 'How many millimetres in 13cm?'

Figure 13.1   'How many millimetres in 13cm?'

It is an excellent opportunity to discuss how the patterns behave and what mathematics underlies the patterns. Noticing and describing these patterns is far closer to the role of a mathematician than repetitive routine practice, no matter how many digits in the numbers.

Assessment

Children can show and explain the patterns they have noticed.

Children can explain how the pattern they found helped them to beat the calculator. Children can reason about the patterns found.

Children can create their own lists of calculation with patterns.

Follow-up tasks

Give the children a mathematical hook, like a catchy riff, or an earworm, or a jingle; find something that lodges in the mind, and set them the task, simply, of noticing it. They could keep a journal, a post-it note, tie a knot in a piece of string every time they hear it, or keep a tally chart on a post-it on their bedroom wall. You need set them nothing more onerous than noticing. If the hook is a good one, then their brains will not be able *not* to notice it.

What should they look for? What makes a good mathematical hook?

- Individual numbers – 11, 13, 99, 75, 101, a dozen, ten, a million, a billion, …

- Number concepts – groups of consecutive numbers, palindromic numbers (121, 4554, 12321, ...), alliterative numbers (forty-four, sixty-seven, two hundred and ten, ...)

- Groups – look out for anything bunched or grouped in fives (fence panels, items in shops, leaves on a twig), or fours, or tens, ...

- Geometric properties – right angles, parallel lines, tessellations, prisms, isosceles triangles, ellipses.

Where should they look? Trust the world – these patterns will come and find you. Watch the news, watch a gameshow, watch a film, play a video game, listen to music, chat to your gran, read a book, go shopping. Just live and have your eyes or ears open.

ACTIVITY

Measured baking

Resources

Any method chosen to record children's baking challenges.

National curriculum and mathematical understanding links

Suitable for: age 5 and above.

Objectives: to notice how mathematics is useful and concrete.

Mathematical understanding: understanding number lines is a key skill in developing a sense of how the operations of addition and subtraction behave dynamically, but the number line is a deceptively complex and profound representation. The number scales used on measuring devices such as tape measures, jugs, thermometers or weighing scales provide concrete variations of the number line, on which children can hang their understanding.

Setting the scene

Baking challenge! Set the challenge of baking bread, biscuits or cake as a class project. Explain that there are going to be very specific measurement criteria to meet, and so the children are going to need to work closely with their families to meet the demands.

Time could be spent in class researching various recipes, taking into account any allergies or healthy-eating considerations. It is not a flippant exercise to undertake, as it demonstrates the role mathematics plays in all aspects of life.

Set the class a challenge that requires measurement in slightly unexpected ways. Some example categories are given below, but the class may very well enjoy creating their own categories:

(Continued)

(Continued)

- Biscuit with a perimeter of 20cm.
- Cake with a top surface of 100cm^2.
- Bread roll that weighs 100g.
- Non-rectangular biscuit with icing demonstrating fifths.

The list could be as inventive or as precise as suits the class. The important point is that children and families engage in discussions about measurements and make decisions together.

Trigger questions

- What do you measure when you cook?
- If you are cooking a cake, what do you need to measure?
- Can you think of any hard recipes to follow? Why are they challenging?
- Can you think of unexpected ways to use measurement when cooking?
- Have you tasted a biscuit with a perimeter of 20cm?

Review and reflect

Discuss all the different measuring that the task required. Children will have used measuring jugs, rulers and weighing scales, and possibly even a thermometer or heat-dial on the oven. Most of these will have used some version of a number line, and this is an excellent source of conversation in class, comparing abstract number lines with the scales used in the kitchen. It may even be appropriate to eat some of the results.

Assessment

Children recognize that the number scales in measuring tools such as a ruler or measuring cup are examples of number lines.

Children can use number scales with different intervals.

Children can compare number lines with different intervals.

Children recognize Lamon's (2012) measurement principles: Compensatory, Approximation and Recursive Partitioning.

Follow-up tasks

Back in class, compare the different measuring activities carried out at home. Alternatively, children can share the final product from their cooking and other children have to figure out what measuring was carried out by their classmate at home.

CONCLUSION

The activities in this chapter are a starting point for engaging parents and carers in mathematical activity with their children. This helps to build children's confidence and enjoyment of exploration, rather than feeling that mathematics is about a rush to the 'right' answer.

REFERENCES

Lamon, **S** (2012) *Teaching Fractions and Ratios for Understanding: Essential Content Knowledge and Instructional Strategies for Teachers*. New York: Routledge.

Mason, **J** and **Johnston-Wilder**, **S** (2005) *Developing Thinking in Geometry*. London: Sage.

FURTHER READING

National Numeracy Family Maths Toolkit. Available at: https://www.nationalnumeracy.org.uk/family-maths-toolkit

14

PREPARING FOR TRANSITION TO SECONDARY MATHEMATICS

MIKE OLLERTON

--- IN THIS CHAPTER ---

This chapter considers the importance of:

- what a primary (Year 6) teacher might do to prepare their students for transition to secondary (Year 7)
- understanding mathematical progression as a seamless transition from primary (Key Stage 2) to secondary (Key Stage 3) rather than a sequence of different steps to be climbed
- journal writing.

The aim of this chapter is to consider ideas that can be taken into any classroom across the Key Stage 2/ Key Stage 3 age range. For each idea/area of content statements from the 2014 National Curriculum programmes of study are identified to illustrate a possible progression. These ideas focus on: Statistics, Fractions, Measurement and Algebra.

Before embarking on the first content area, it is worth reminding ourselves of the three main aims of the national curriculum for mathematics. These are fluency, reasoning and solving problems. These aims can be linked to seminal mathematics reports such as Cockcroft (1982):

The primary mathematics curriculum should enrich children's aesthetic and linguistic experience, provide them with the means of exploring their environment and develop their powers of logical thought, in addition to equipping them with the numerical skills which will be a powerful tool for later work and study.

(para 287)

and HMI (1985):

Mathematics is not an arbitrary collection of disconnected items, but has a coherent structure in which the various parts are inter-related. In very simple terms mathematics is about relationships. For example, there are relationships between any two numbers which may be expressed in different forms: 18 may be said to be greater than 6, or 12 more than 6 …

(para 1.4)

Any task presented to learners needs to provide opportunities for exploration, logic and seeking relationships while at the same time developing skills and content knowledge. Creating opportunities for learners to develop reasoning skills underpins their content knowledge development; knowing why something works the way it does as well as how something works is a key component of learning. This links to Skemp's (1976) seminal article on relational understanding and instrumental understanding.

The chapter ends by making a case for journal writing, where Year 6 learners can take with them two or three pieces of mathematics that represents their 'best' achievements.

STATISTICS

The first activity is about statistics. The statutory requirements in Year 4, Year 6 and Key Stage 3 are:

- Year 4 – interpret and present discrete and continuous data using appropriate graphical methods, including bar charts and time graphs

- Year 6 – interpret and construct pie charts and line graphs and use these to solve problems (and) calculate and interpret the mean as an average

- Key Stage 3 – describe, interpret and compare observed distributions of a single variable through: appropriate graphical representation involving discrete, continuous and grouped data; and appropriate measures of central tendency (mean, mode, median) and spread (range, consideration of outliers).

ACTIVITY

Using an image to prompt estimation

Project a copy of a star sheet (Figure 14.1) onto a whiteboard for no more than a few seconds; indeed, having the image on screen as children are entering the room can be a potentially useful strategy to grab their attention; to add a little 'mystery' to the start of a lesson.

(Continued)

(Continued)

Figure 14.1   Star sheet (Ollerton, 2002)

Once everyone has seen the image, switch off the screen and ask the students to write an estimate of the number of stars on a post-it note, together with their initials. These estimates are recorded (a spreadsheet is a good tool for this as it allows easy analysis of the data linking well with the Computing curriculum) with results usually ranging from 30 to 100.

Then pose the question: 'How can we use this information to try to arrive at an agreed class answer to how many stars there are?'

Giving time for groups of learners to discuss this question to agree on different ways to gain an agreed class answer is usually very interesting.

Grouped frequency charts can be drawn and this will depend upon the data collected; clearly issues about the range of estimates and how the data might be grouped will provide further useful discussion.

To deepen learners' statistical knowledge, we can try the following: return the original post-it notes to the learners, then, in light of the work they have completed from the first set of estimates, ask them to write a second estimate on their post-it note. These can be re-collected and the information added to the earlier data set.

Initials	First estimate	Second estimate
AJ	47	71
GB	82	60
etc.	etc.	etc.

All the different types of analyses and charts drawn from the first set of estimates can be repeated for the second set and comparisons can be drawn between the two data sets; in addition, learners could plot a scatter graph to see if anything of interest emerges.

Depending on children's previous experience, it might be appropriate to discuss mean, median and mode. It might also be useful to see how close, or not, they are to the actual number of stars by finding the value halfway between the two outliers.

It might also be worth going back to the image and seeing how good their estimates were. What strategies could be used to count all the stars?

What other questions might be asked about this image?

When do you get asked to estimate in everyday life? For example, 'How many pennies/sweets in a jar at a fund-raising event?', 'Will this fit here?', 'Is there enough for ...?'

Returning to the Key Stage 3 statutory requirements, we can see each element being 'catered' for, such as graphical interpretations of data, averages, range and outliers.

Pedagogically, I see such a task as one of ownership, where the learners create and analyse their own data; this is distinctly and fundamentally different to presenting them with ready-made data in the form of a worksheet or a textbook exercise.

FRACTIONS

The next activity is about fractions. As above, it is important for the Year 6 teacher to know how the learning of fractions progresses from Key Stage 1. One thread of the statutory requirements relating to fractions appears as follows in Year 2, Year 4 and Year 6:

- Year 2 - recognize, find and name a half as one of two equal parts of an object, shape or quantity (and similarly for a quarter)

- Year 4 - recognize and show, using diagrams, families of common equivalent fractions

- Year 5 - identify, name and write equivalent fractions of a given fraction, represented visually, including tenths and hundredths

- Year 6 - add and subtract fractions with different denominators and mixed numbers, using the concept of equivalent fractions.

ACTIVITY

Shapes and paper

Many Year 2 children will be encouraged to cut shapes into two equal size pieces, such as rectangles (which includes squares) and triangles. This task begins by folding any A-size piece of paper

(Continued)

(Continued)

by joining a pair of opposite corners together and can easily be extended to challenge children across primary and beyond. This creates a fold line as shown in Figure 14.2:

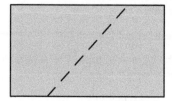

Figure 14.2 Creating a fold line

Now cut along the fold to give a pair of congruent quadrilaterals. What type of quadrilateral is it? Why?

By joining equal edge lengths together, different shapes can be made (Figure 14.3). How can you be sure that you have found them all? Convince yourself, convince a friend, convince a teacher.

Figure 14.3 Creating different shapes by joining equal edge lengths

For each shape, depending on age and experience, children can discuss the number of edges, the symmetry properties, the perimeter (you can label the lengths of the original quadrilateral a, b, c and d to assist with this). In this way, work on fractions can be connected to geometry, algebra and counting.

Paper folding is a powerful way of experiencing equivalent fractions.

Give pairs of children different coloured strips of paper each the same length. Challenge them to fold their strips into halves, thirds, quarters, etc. This will allow children to experience the halving connections between halves, quarters and eighths. Similarly, by halving thirds we gain sixths. Folding into fifths and sevenths will be more of a challenge but this is all the more reason for posing such tasks.

The folded strips can be arranged in a fraction wall, but this is a fraction wall with a difference, where strips are placed as a series of number lines, from 0 to 1 (Figure 14.4).

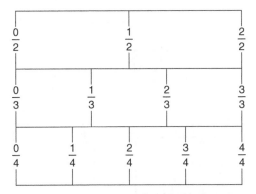

Figure 14.4   Series of number lines in a fraction wall

If strips of folded paper go down to, say, twelfths, then equivalence classes will emerge.

A further challenge would be to write the fractional amount in order. Figure 14.5 shows a Year 5 learner's work showing fraction strips up to sixths.

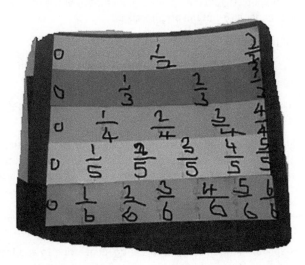

Figure 14.5   A Year 5 learner's work showing fraction strips up to sixths

(Continued)

(Continued)

Adding fractions with different denominators is something much older children in Key Stage 3 and in Key Stage 4 have been known to struggle with. For this reason, it is all the more important to take time and give Upper Key Stage 2 children practical experiences that can lead to an understanding of how to add (and subtract) fractions without the teacher telling them a procedure.

Give each learner a piece of A5 paper and ask them to fold it into thirds across the short side and into quarters across the long side. This will produce 12 twelfths as in Figure 14.6.

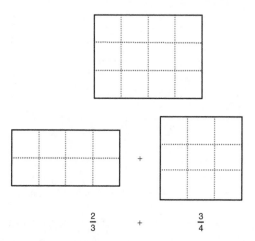

$$\frac{2}{3} \qquad + \qquad \frac{3}{4}$$

Figure 14.6   Folding paper into thirds and quarters

The next task is to ask one pupil to fold their piece of paper into $\frac{2}{3}$ of the original size and their partner to fold their piece of paper into $\frac{3}{4}$ of the original size.

Using the two pieces of paper we have:

Given the pupil holding the $\frac{2}{3}$ size will automatically have $\frac{8}{12}$ and the pupil with the $\frac{3}{4}$ will have $\frac{9}{12}$, the answer $\frac{17}{12} = 1\frac{5}{12}$ cannot be too far away from being realized.

The same process can be used for carrying out subtraction, so $\frac{3}{4} - \frac{2}{3}$ becomes $\frac{9}{12} - \frac{8}{12}$, producing the required answer of $\frac{1}{12}$.

Various challenges can now be provided such as making up all possible addition calculations using quarters and thirds. If the same kind of challenge were to be applied to subtraction, it would be interesting to see if anybody recognized that to calculate $\frac{2}{3} - \frac{3}{4}$ would, in fact, produce a negative fractional answer.

In Key Stage 3, fractions appear in many contexts: ordering, converting to and from decimals, as a percentage change, as algebraic coefficients, expressing proportions and ratios. As such, the task above requires learners to both take their time and to be given plenty of time, allowing them to explore how the same paper-folding approach can be used with a range of fractions, halves and thirds, halves and fifths, thirds and fifths, quarters and fifths.

Pedagogically, I intend children to develop fluency and to reason about how to add and subtract pairs of fractions, with different denominators *without* the teacher telling them a fixed procedure; instead to see, for themselves, what is 'going on'.

MEASUREMENT AND ALGEBRA

I combine these two areas of the curriculum, starting first with algebra and then offering a task connected to algebra in the context of mensuration.

One route to algebra is through finding missing numbers in number sentences. After all, there are only small, cognitive steps from:

$5 + \square = 8$ to

$5 + ? = 8$ to

$5 + x = 8$

The first equation with a missing number denoted by $\square$ was the starting point for a lesson in which children generated their own calculations then replaced some of the numbers with blank rectangles as a problem for their peers.

ACTIVITY

Missing number problems

The children wrote their missing number problems on brightly coloured sheets of A5 paper, together with their name and stuck them up around the classroom. As soon as everyone had displayed at least two problems, children went round the room trying to solve each other's problems.

$$3 \times (\square - 2) + \square = 25$$

Children had chosen what level of difficulty they wanted to work at: addition or subtraction using 2-digit, 3-digit or 4-digit numbers, multiplication or division calculations.

One child made up a missing number problem using Roman numerals. Oh, the joy of seeing such creative thinking!

Interestingly, there was a governors' meeting that evening and the head teacher, insisted they had to solve some of the children's missing number problems before the meeting could begin.

In the next lesson, we worked on missing numbers in calculations involving dimensions of rectangles together with areas and perimeters. This involved:

* drawing a rectangle on squared paper
* calculating the area and the perimeter of the rectangle

(Continued)

(Continued)

- as previously, transferring just some of the information, onto a brightly coloured piece of A5 paper and adding their name
- sticking the problem on the wall for others to tackle.

We looked at different degrees of difficulty so the children could decide for themselves what they wanted to make up questions about. These were:

- knowing the two dimensions and leaving the area and the perimeter blank
- knowing one dimension and the area and leaving the other dimension and the perimeter blank
- knowing one dimension and the perimeter and leaving the other dimension and the area blank
- knowing the area and the perimeter and leaving both dimensions blank.

Three examples from children in Year 3, Year 5 and Year 6 are shown in Figure 14.7.

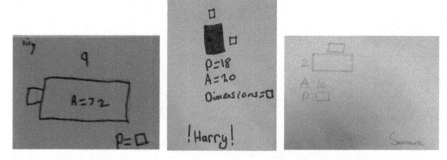

Figure 14.7   Year 3, 5 and 6 learner's rectangle dimensions, area and perimeter problems

In the following lesson some children created 'harder' problems having seen similar ones their peers had made up; these children, in turn, created problems on compound shapes and this led to discussions about what missing numbers such shapes could have.

Later, several children wrote missing number problems involving sequences; some even went into negative values.

INTERCONNECTEDNESS OF MATHEMATICS

This activity connects geometry, fractions and algebra. It is one I have used with a Year 3 to Year 6 class, Year 7 and Year 8 classes; with the Key Stage 3 classes I presented a variation of the initial starting point by using four triangles with areas of $\frac{1}{2}, \frac{1}{4}, \frac{1}{8}$ and $\frac{1}{8}$.

ACTIVITY

Shapes

With the Year 3 to Year 6 class I began with a square piece of card dissected into three pieces; a three-piece tangram, as in Figure 14.8:

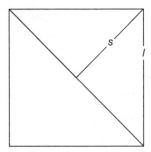

Figure 14.8   Three-piece tangram

This activity involves making shapes using both two and three pieces.

After giving children time to explore and to ask questions about the names of the shapes, a next question could be to try to find a complete collection of shapes; to 'prove' they have not missed any out. This, of course requires some form of reasoning.

JOURNAL WRITING

At the 2010 British Congress of Mathematics Education conference, a keynote speaker asked the audience two questions. The first was (I paraphrase): 'What does an art student take with them to the next stage?' (from GCSE to A-level, from A-level to college or university, from college or from university to the world of work). The answer is 'a portfolio'. The second question was: 'What does a Mathematics student take with them?' The answer is a grade. These questions stuck with me because they reminded me of how, when I was a 'proper' teacher I would ask my learners to produce portfolios of the best pieces of mathematics they had worked on.

I believe one way to deepen cognition is to cause learners to write about the mathematics they have worked on. This would include drawing pictures, graphs and charts (tables). One reason for writing journals is to intentionally slow learners down by considering what all their 'doing' actually means in terms of what mathematics they have understood/made sense of. A journal could be a compilation of paper and electronically based evidence and may include a presentation or poster they can present to their peers.

I am not suggesting learners write about every piece of mathematics they do. I want them to reflect upon and write about problems they have worked on successfully or about some mathematics they feel they have really understood.

Year 6 learners could consider their new Year 7 mathematics teacher as the audience for their writing. The journal will provide a rich addition to their National Curriculum Test score.

CONCLUSION

This chapter considers key issues about:

a. progression, both in terms of transition from Key Stage 2 to Key Stage 3 and curriculum progression; and how ideas for classrooms can be extended in order to deepen children's conceptual knowledge

b. teaching and learning different areas of the curriculum, for example, statistics, fractions and measurement and algebra in ways that nurture problem solving, reasoning and conceptual understanding

c. the power of journal writing as a medium for learners to present and reflect on mathematics they have enjoyed and understood.

Implicit throughout a) and b) are issues of the interconnectedness of mathematics and optimizing access to mathematics for all learners. This means removing artificial ceilings for their achievements so children are more likely to value and enjoy what they do. As expressed in a note from a Year 4 child:

> Thank you for a wonderful lesson I had soooooo much fun meshureing (sic) people hope you had a good time

REFERENCES

Cockcroft Report (1982) *Mathematics Counts*. London: HMSO.

HMI (1985) 'Mathematics from 5 to 16', HMI Series: *Curriculum Matters*, No.3, London: HMSO.

Ollerton, M (2002) *Learning and teaching mathematics without a textbook*, Derby: Association of Teachers of Mathematics.

Skemp, R (1976) 'Relational understanding and instrumental understanding', *Mathematics Teaching*, 77: 20-26.

Wolfe, C (2013) 'Maths journals and my experiment with Y7', *Mathematics Teaching*, 234.

INDEX